THE LION

OF

THE TRIBE OF JUDAH

By
Tella Olayeri
+2348023583168

All rights reserved. No part of this publication may be reproduced, stored in a retrieval system or transmitted in any form or by any means electronics, mechanical, photocopying, recording, or otherwise, without the prior written permission of the publisher, in accordance with the provisions of the copyright Act.

Any person who does any unauthorized act in relation to this publication may be liable to criminal prosecution and civil claims for damages. It is protected under the copyright laws.

Published By:
GOD'S LINK VENTURES

Email tellaolayeri@gmail.com

Website www.tellaolayeri.com

Blog www.tellaolayeri.com/blog

US Contact

TELLA OLAYERI

Ruth Jack

14 Milewood Road

Verbank

N.Y.12585

U.S.A. +19176428989

All texts, calls, letters, testimonies and enquiries are welcome.

CONNECT WITH US

WHATSAPP

Every Saturday we connect through zoom to pray in solidarity. We have a WhatsApp group to easily communicate about the Zoom meetings and other important updates. I'd appreciate, if you click the link below to join the WhatsApp group to always notify you.

https://tellaolayeri.com/resources.php

FACEBOOK

(Like and follow our page)

https://web.facebook.com/tellaolayeri/

(Join our Facebook Group)

Do you want your dream interpreted, do you need powerful morning and night prayers that command breakthrough, healing and favour.

Join my Facebook group today and receive testimony.

https://web.facebook.com/groups/tellaolayeri

INSTAGRAM

https://www.instagram.com/tellaolayeri/

TWITTER

https://twitter.com/tellaolayeri

DEDICATION

This book is dedicated to the **HOLY GHOST** for inspiring me to write this eye opening book.

APPRECIATION

My appreciation goes to my dedicated wife, **MRS NGOZI OLAYERI,** who typed the manuscript of this book and designed the cover page. My darling wife I say thank you. My appreciation equally goes to my lovely children, **MISS IBUKUN, DAVID, MICHAEL COMFORT and MERCY.** They encouraged me day and night as I write this book

Respect and honor should be given to who is due. Favor comes from God and men as well. My calling (writing evangelism) met the timely support of a particular man of God, preacher, teacher, prophet and General Overseer. He awakes my inner man and gave me sound spiritual support. Without his earlier support for my first book, <u>**Fire for Fire Prayer Book**</u> and subsequent ones, I may not be where I am today in Christian literature writing. He gallantly stood by me in fulfillment of my calling.

This book you are holding is a testimony of my claim. This book wouldn't have seen the light of the day, if not for the spiritual encouragement I gathered from my father in the Lord who served as spiritual mirror that brightens my hope to explore my calling.

I am talking of no any other person than the **General Overseer of MOUNTAIN OF FIRE AND MIRACLES MINISTRIES WORLD WIDE, DR. D. K. OLUKOYA.**

Once again, I say thank you sir. Your support has yielded yet another earth shaking book.

THANKS.
Evangelist Tella Olayeri.

PREFACE

You are important before God right from the day of creation. The fall of Adam and Eve in the garden as a result of serpent's deception made we inherit struggles in the course of our journey on planet earth. The mistake happened and Jesus came as the Second Adam to put things straight for us. In the course of this the spirit of Lion of Judah came to be. This is a heavenly spirit of Jesus Christ to strengthen and empower us against the devices of Satan.

This book give details of spirit of Lion of Judah fighting battles for us, give solution to problem and the challenges we encounter. God knows us more than we know ourselves. The hair of our head is numbered and our name is on his palm. This means we are his children unless we sell our soul to Satan. It is a matter of choice. This is where the spirit of Lion of Judah comes in. People ruled by this spirit become great and wonderful in life.

They are not ignored in heaven because of the intimacy with the supernatural.

This book teaches us how to manage economy of life to transfigure us and glow. Where you are today is what you saw yesterday and what you said yesterday. Nobody made it available to you, you created today what you see and by what you use. But if you are impregnated with spirit of Lion of Judah your understanding will explode. What you will do in two days ahead is brought to fruition today; and you do it well. This is Lion of Judah's spirit synergy. The Lord is there for you to conquer more territory.

This is a marvelous book that will make you capture your environment. The reason the devil appears very strong is that our ignorance empowers him. You are guided on how to remove the ignorance and make devil helpless. You remain focus in the Lord and avoid every manner of distraction.

The Lord wants you to occupy position of Jesus on earth with a ruler's staff in hand and control your situation. He wants your feet to walk and occupy places and dominate. A man with spirit of Lion of Judah builds hope, have hope and exercise hope to fruition. Confidence is built and results achieved.

With this book the Lord will turn your wailing into dancing and remove garment that bring you low. Weep may remain for a night, you will surely rejoice at the end as mountains disappear and barriers break. The lion of Judah is at work. You will have cause to praise God, our refuge that never put us to shame. He is our rock of refuge, a strong fortress and a strong tower.

This book is loaded with powerful prayers vomited by the Holy Spirit to enjoy the followings:

THE LION OF THE TRIBE OF JUDAH

1. You are empowered to explore the world to maximum opportunity to soar and make good harvest in life.
2. This book will develop your intimacy with God in the sphere of life to plant, to harvest and to dismantle evil plantations that may stand as barrier to your breakthrough.
3. The spirit of lion you apply in the book enables you possess dominion and authority and put the enemies under your feet.
4. The spirit of lion that resides in you kill spirit that makes you sin unconsciously. Your heart is repositioned, healed and active to God.
5. You will be liberated from the grip of Goliath, that steal and kill, that enslave and destroy harvest of greatness and cause fear of captivity.
6. Your prayer style improves while windows of opportunity open wide.
7. You will discover the D.N.A of Jesus in you that you never use. His D.N.A enables you to occupy territory of wonders and miracles.

Scores of victory awaits you. Receive them by fire.

GOOD NEWS!!!

My audiobook is now available, to get one visit **audible**.

If you are reading from my paperback visit **acx.com** and search **"Tella Olayeri."**

Brethren, to be loaded and reloaded visit**:** **amazon.com/author/tellaolayeri** for a full spiritual sojourn for my books.

Thanks.

PREVIOUS PUBLICATIONS OF THE AUTHOR

Before we proceed, I'd like to say thank you for downloading this book. I believe the information in it will bless your life greatly. Please find below other books that God has empowered me write. They are meant to be a blessing to your life and family.

See all at: **amazon.com/author/tellaolayeri**

Or at other bookstore at

https://tellaolayeri.com/pointofsale.php or **https://books2read.com/tellaolayeri**

THE LION OF THE TRIBE OF JUDAH

Table of Contents

CHRISTIAN COUNSELLING 17

THE SPIRIT OF LION OF JUDAH 18

WARFARE LIONS IN THE SCHOOL OF PRAYER 56

THE WARRIORS OF CHRIST IN HEAVEN 97

HOW TO WALK IN THE SUPERNATURAL 122

THE ANOINTING OF THE HOLY SPIRIT 154

THANKSGIVING IN THE MOUTH OF LIONS 178

DONATE TO THE MINISTRY 220

CHRISTIAN COUNSELLING

The world is full of mystery. We need answers to navigate difficult situations that confront us. We provide tools and insights in prayer and counselling to see far and wide to fulfill your destiny.

Our counselling is broad in prayer, dream interpretations, and other enquires. For detail, click the link to know when I will be available.

https://calendly.com/tellaolayeri

CHAPTER 1

THE SPIRIT OF LION OF JUDAH

The spirit of Lion of Judah is a download from heaven to equip and set you free of forces that keep you back. We forge ahead in spirit if we tap from the supernatural realm and engage in full measure. In the beginning our D.N.A is God when he said, ***"Let us make man in our image, after our likeness…"*** **Genesis 1:26.** No creation enjoy such privilege but Adam. It was lost in the Garden of Eden when the serpent double crossed Adam's intelligence by eating the forbidden fruit. The spirit of Lion of Judah is traced to Jesus who came to our rescue. He was God in flesh and close to God. Jesus is called the Lion of Judah who triumphed over death and sin. Jesus triumphed over temptation and sin, over pain and suffering, over fear, over death and over the Devil himself.

God knows us better. **He said to Jeremiah, *"Before I formed you in the womb I knew you, before you were born I set you apart; I appointed you as a prophet to the nations"*. Jeremiah 1:5.** This confirms he knows us, knows our capacity in strength, weakness, opportunities and threats we shall face in the journey of life. We lost in the Garden through the first Adam and empowered in the second Adam; Jesus Christ of Nazareth. Until we operate in the supernatural we know nothing. He taught us how to fast, and how to focus heaven for answer. He is the Lion at all times and we rely on him to operate in the supernatural.

It is when possessed with Lion's spirit we download God. The prayer of the righteous avails much. If you live a holy life and willing to pray part of the job is done. If you can't pray, you are not part of what God is doing. The doctrine of blessing is deeper and powerful than giving and receiving. Christians that don't understand the principle of intelligence interaction is not relevant in this term.

The book of **Isaiah 40:28 says, *"Do you not know? Have you not heard? The Lord is the everlasting God, the creator of the ends of the earth. He will not grow tired or weary, and his understanding no one can fathom"*.** He is far and wide above us. He knows all things. He is willing to accept us, if we determine to operate in the supernatural. God did not promise them bread and wine nor job opportunity, but should learn the act of the supernatural to mount up wings and be supernatural in thinking in financial intelligence and technologies. At this point they soar on wings like eagles ready for business because they hope in the Lord. This is the account ***"But those who hope in the Lord will renew their strength. They will soar on wings like eagles; they will run and not grow weary, they will work and not be faint"***

Isaiah 40:51. They soar, because the Spirit of the Lion of Judah dwells in them.

What happens at this point? The spirit of lion of Judah in you empowers you to mingle with divinity until you become express representation of the dimension of invisible God. You must pray to the point you become expression of God. The rule is "They that become economy of prayer will rule". When you pray there is no way you can be defeated. You become host of God. There is a dimension your life represents but you need to host God. Our growth depends on the quality of prayer. Heaven is a place to explore if you allow the spirit of Lion of Judah to operate in you. Heaven is a place to explore, if you saturate with God and doors begin to open.

Everything in the physical is a product of spiritual download. There is territorial energy that regulates your choices. When you don't have encounter with God, your job will define you, your environment will define you, the food you eat will define you, the cloth you wear will define you. But, when the Lion in you appears or resurrects from sleep, you control your environment. It is when you are a Lion, you won't sell yourself cheap to people. You won't be deflowered before marriage. It is when you are a lion in Christ as a medical doctor, you won't specialize in the trade of abortion; or tell lies to win cases as a lawyer in the law court.

You won't be rubbished by the enemy if you download the heavenly into your situation. This is what makes you a lion in the spirit. The more you allow the spirit of lion operate in you the stronger you are in the Lord. You grow in the spirit and never go down. Do you know why? It is because you are specially purchased with currency of the blood of Jesus, the author of life and King of the lion of the tribe of Judah. The blood of Jesus transfigured you to a special being that can't be rubbished by the enemy. The Lord paid a price for you on the cross. When saturated with the blood you are a spirit being in Jesus. If you are evaluated, it will be on the blood of Jesus. Except you discover yourself in God you will never attain your full potential.

The spirit of lion in you develops your intimacy with God and makes you hear him. God's voice is not loud but distinct. If you can't distinguish voice of God, he will speak and you won't pick. You will think it is your mind-set or someone else. It is the spirit in you that will let you discern the voice of God. Jesus said my sheep hears my voice. My sheep understands what I say. My sheep can distinguish my voice from others. You can't give command to sheep that is not yours or in charge. If you are a stranger, it won't obey you. As sheep obeys you, you will obey God if you have intimacy with him. The spirit of Lion tells the intimacy you carry. It removes the veil between you and God. To hear God, separate yourself apart to God and wait. Your voice is recognized in heaven. If my wife calls me with strange number, I will know her voice. The reason we don't hear God's voice is that we don't spend time with him.

You are a prey to predator if you can't hear from God. If spirit of the Lion of Judah operates in you and predator comes you will know and it will fail. Spend time with God if you want to hear from him. Many times the distance between life and death is a whisper. Some year ago, I went to park to travel. On arrival the vehicle to load has two passengers to complete. I told them I want to relax before I pay. One man came and paid. If I pay the vehicle will move. Then the driver call my attention to pay, I told him I am not ready. As we talk, a man arrived, paid and the vehicle left. I have to wait for the next vehicle. We were there for another two hours. The passengers of the vehicle complete and we move. On the way we saw the first vehicle in a deep pit. The driver was involved in a ghastly accident. All passengers died. The reason I refuse to enter the vehicle was I heard a voice that says, "Don't travel with this vehicle. Death, death, is coming". The reason was eventually confirmed. Allow spirit of God to control you. It is the spirit of the Lion of tribe of Judah.

Prophet Elijah was embodied with spirit of the Lion of Judah when he commanded the widow to collect empty vessels and fill it with oil. The extent you can receive is directly proportional to the magnitude to your expectation. He said to the woman gather vessel, gather not a few, because he knew that when the vessels are filled the oil will stop flowing. And so it is important for you to enlarge the boundary of your heart to receive the spirit of Lion of Judah which opens doors of greatness. Focus God, his name is EL-Shadai the multi blessed one. There is no scarcity in his realm. There is no depletion in his realm. How much you can receive is a function of the allocated space you made available.

Open your heart to receive from God. Everything is created by him. Even if he did not create he is still God. This is enough to let you open your heart to let spirit of Lion of Judah abide in you to receive from God. There are things that are gift in God's kingdom and things that are rewards. God is multi-blessed. There are many dimensions in personality called God. There are many things in God we can't understand. All that is allocated to God is complete in Christ. Jesus is to give you what pertained to life and Godliness. Even though you are dead in sin and sin require penalty for forgiveness to be prosecuted. On the strength of his love he became a sin offering. He took verdict of death so that you can receive eternal life. On the strength of this, it is an error for you to be poor, because he became poor for you to be rich. On the strength of this, it is an error for you to struggle.

Everything God has, he makes available for you because you are an heir of Christ and you approach his kingdom with the spirit of the Lion of Judah.

When Jesus was young, he sat with elders in the synagogue. He did not jump the gun. He listened to elders; gradually building spiritual quality life. The spirit of Lion of Judah in him awakes. Also, he learned carpentry, the professional calling of his earthly father Joseph. There are many things he learned along the line. There are people in Africa today that want to escape to other countries to seek greener pasture. How do you know you must leave your country before you make it? Your destiny may be Africa. The question is, if you are a Lizard in Africa, what tells you, you will be a crocodile in U.K or Europe, Canada or U.S.A? If you get there it may take you five years or more before you get work permit. This years you wasted may be the years that will equip you to great height as Jesus before he started his ministry. But if the spirit of

Lion resides in you, it may be time of God's elevation. You allow anxiety if you go to a place you call greener pasture. In fact, abroad doesn't mean pasture is available. This was the error of Mr. Lot when he choose where leads to Sodom and Gomorrah that ends up in flames. Let the spirit of Lion of Judah in you dictate not flesh.

The spirit of Lion of Judah makes you a prayer warrior and commander in the spirit. You are fearless like Daniel who prayed three times a day against the decree of the king. He was arrested and locked in the den of lions hoping he will die. Prayer turned his posture to a Lion. He was a Lion in the spirit like other carnivorous Lions in the hole. They became friends. What the Lions saw was not Daniel but a new visitor in the like of a Lion. Lion doesn't hurt Lion. The rule was followed to the letter and Daniel was spared through the hands of God.

This is the reason you must be a prayer warrior. We have 168 hours in a week. How many hours do you pray in a week that may turn you to a Lion? This is the question every Christian should answer. In a year of 8,736 hours, how many hours do you pray in a year? Jesus fasted and prayed for 960 hours yet Satan came after him. He won because he was a Lion from the tribe of Judah. In fact, Jesus was the Lion. No wonder Jesus rebuked him, "Get behind me Satan", which means, Satan get lost! Satan you are defeated! Satan, disappear by fire! Satan, I march upon you. You will march over Satan, in the name of Jesus.

The temptation of Jesus was a stepping stone to Jesus glory. Jesus was loaded with spirit of Lion of Judah. Though he was in the spirit, he dramatized it in the physical. Satan said, "Turn this stone to bread". He overcame it by the Word. Satan said, "Bow down and worship me". Jesus overcame him by the Word. Satan failed. He failed because there was spirit of lion in him that travailed the day.

The spirit of Jesus was incubated with spirit of a Lion. The Bible says, ***"Jesus returned to Galilee in the power of the Spirit, and news about him spread through the whole country side"***. **Luke 4:14.** I pray your fasting and prayer will not be in vain, in the name of Jesus. You energize your spirit when you pray and fast.

The spirit of Lion of Judah makes you bold. When Jesus was arrested and was to be crucified. The bible says, in **Luke 23:27-28;** ***"A large number of people followed him, including women who mourned and wailed for him. Jesus turned and said to them, "Daughters of Jerusalem, do not weep for me: weep for yourselves and for your children"***. The spirit of Lion in him cleared the fear.

The spirit was in him even when he was crucified. On crucifixion ground Jesus roared like a Lion and shouted, *"It is finished"* **John 19:30.** I extend it to you in prayer. Every problem in your life is finished, in the name of Jesus. Every shame and disgrace in your life is finished in the name of Jesus. Also, I pray, you are redeemed and today start your day of salvation. You will experience eternal life because Jesus fought the battle and won. It is finished in **Greek means TETELESTAI.**

The spirit of Lion of Judah turns you to celestial personnel. As Jesus prayed in Gethsemane his composure changed. The sweat on him was like blood. The disciples were surprised. They couldn't go close to him. He was a changed man. Moses and Elijah came to him to deliver the great message. He knew his arrest before he descended mount Gethsemane. The Lion in him roared and he became a changed man. He feared no arrest. He was bold and fearless to the end. May the spirit of Lion of Judah encompass you now and forever more; Amen

The spirit of Lion of Judah is a spirit of thunder. When Paul encountered Jesus, a light like thunder strike. He fell and scale covered his face. He could not see for three days. Paul said the language he heard was Hebrew but others around him heard different language. The spirit of Lion arrested Paul and was deposited in Him. No wonder he was bold, fearless, intelligent and radical in ministry. You need such spirit. He has inner eyes that see, spiritual ears that hears and heavenly heart that understands. The hands of Paul became machine hands of letter. He wrote more than everyone in the Bible. The spirit of Lion of Judah reigned in him. Pray for spirit that explodes destiny till eternity.

When there is challenge God sends his anointed. When information is to be passed he sent his own.

The person sent is loaded with spirit to unravel answer to the situation. He that God sent carry's the Spirit of Lion of Judah. He sees challenge and solves it. The Apostles were filled with Holy Spirit after Jesus ascended to heaven. Ananias lay hands and speaks to the life of Paul before he could receive his sight. Phillip guides the Eunuch of the passage of book of Isaiah he was reading and baptized him and the spirit of the Lord carried Phillip away. The spirit of Lion of Judah empowers you to experience extra-ordinary.

The three Hebrew boys, **Shadrach, Meshach, and Abednego,** received spirit of Lion of Judah when they declared they won't bow to idol. In the midst of threat, they preferred to be casted into fire heated seven times than normal. The flame was fearful while they were filled with boldness. They stood their ground as the fire pour out fear. It never bothered them. Also, the Lion of Judah himself was waiting for them in the fire. No one saw him.

Nobody envisaged it. As they were pushed to the fearful fire, the story changed. The fire was air conditioned by God. It became pleasantry to them, guess what? The fourth man appeared in the fire. They were four in number. The king saw the fourth man in the fire. He was surprised. They clapped hands and danced round in the fire. The spirit of Lion of Judah takes over. They were later replaced by their accusers and the Lion in the fire disappear. The angel finished his assignment. It is good to be loaded with spirit of Lion of Judah to silence works of darkness and enemy of progress. I pray your enemy will pay the price of their handwork in the name of Jesus.

To deny God is evil. To deny God is unrighteousness. Mr. Job avoided both in the book of Job. Though he was in pain and sorrow, he didn't deny God. His condition was precarious but was equipped with spirit of God. The spirit of Lion dwelled in him. He encourage himself to hold back curse of God despite being infected with sores, losses and infirmities. The battle was between the Lion of Judah in Job and Satan. The voice of Job is liken to Esther, when she said, "If I perish I perish". This is heavenly language spoken by men and women that are Lions and Lioness in the spirit.

Lions are kings in the Jungle. They fear no animal. The roar of Lion makes other animals tremble. People that go to forest to pray are Lions in the jungle of Christ. Those who go to the wilderness to pray are like Jesus in the making. Abraham was called out of his father's house and was on a journey he never knew the place he was going. He became lion in the spirit the day he stepped out of his father's house because wild animals that consume were along the way he took. But, because he was a lion in the spirit no wild animal attacked him. They knew there boundary. He was surrounded by enemy and unfriendly friends, the good and bad people yet he overcame them all. He summoned courage like a Lion and left his father's house. His great grandchild Jacob pronounced on Judah, "You are the Lion of Judah", when he assembled his children before him and blessed them. Abraham built the foundation of Lion of Judah; Jacob confirmed it. What looks like fear or uncertainty to Abraham became ladder of greatness to his grandchild Jacob. May the spirit of Lion of Judah do wonders in your life; amen

Moses was a wanted man in Egypt. The palace sought to kill him and he fled. He fled to an unknown land where God appeared to him. He was ordered to go back to Egypt to set Israel free. He feared to do it, knowing well his past record. The Lion in him arose; he marched to the palace in Egypt and declared to Pharaoh, "The Lord says, let my people go". He was bold to say it like a Lion. Moses knew he was to walk through the valley of death, he feared no evil. He knew the rod in his hand shall be the rod of God.

The spirit of Goliath is a spirit that wastes life. It is a spirit that boasts. It is a spirit assign to kill and destroy. It is a spirit that enslaves people and denies them harvest. It is a spirit that believes in other gods to Yahweh. It is a spirit that count days, months or years to enslave victim. It is a spirit everybody fears. It takes one with heart of a Lion to conquer such spirit. You must be bold as David to bring down such a spirit or power. Summon courage today, awake the Lion in you. Let it roar like thunder and by fire.

It is the spirit of Lion of Judah that makes you acknowledge futility of life. Your spirit won't allow you accumulate unjust wealth. The spirit won't allow you boast of the number of cars you have in the carriage, the number of houses you build, the amount in your bank account, the number of your children etc. You are judged by where you occupy in the supernatural realm. This is what speaks for you. You are possessed with the spirit of the Lion of Judah the day you realize that everything on earth shall be consumed by fire. ***"Seeing then that all these things shall be dissolved, what manner of persons ought ye to be in all holy conversation and godliness, looking for and hasting unto the coming of the day of God, wherein the heavens being on fire shall be dissolved, and the elements shall melt with fervent heat?"*** **2 Peter 3:11-12.**

The day you come to your senses moths shall eat what you labor for and gathered, is the day lion of Judah dwells in you. The day you know this, is the day spirit of Lion of Judah arrests you to God. From that day, you won't follow what looks appealing to the eyes but heaven. You will build your treasure in heaven. Nothing appeals to you on earth. This is handwork of spirit of Lion of Judah.

The Lord understands you better than you do. He knew the children of Israel are weak. They stayed long in bondage and it mastered them. Though they cry to God, their heart did not leave Egypt. They feared war as well. They never tested war before. To them Goshen was paradise. God knew this; he led them by the way of the Red Sea, though short cut to the Promised Land was available. God said, if they saw war they will turn back to Egypt. The Lion in them was still a baby or a sleeping giant. The Lord made them see the stubborn pursuers after them, yet they were not consumed. The Red Sea consumed the stubborn pursuers after them. The Lion in them arose and they believe in God. Moses re-kindles the fire in him and marched forward with the spirit of a lion.

The spirit of Lion of Judah enveloped Moses when he descended from mount Horeb. His eyes were like fire. The multitude could not look at his eyes. The hands of God were upon Him. This is how it is, to people that fast 30, 40, 50,100 days or more. They are different mankind. Elijah spoke and fire fall. Isaiah encountered God and his tongue became tongue of fire when the angel put coal of fire in his tongue. His eyes open and became a different man. Today; the Lion in you shall arise and you will be a changed man.

It is not your preaching that makes you a known person; you are not the best preacher. That you are an author of many titles doesn't make you popular, it is God that advertises men. Many wrote like Paul, they are not known. You need the spirit of a Lion to keep you afloat. You need the spirit that will anoint you to have impact on people. The spirit must arrest you before you fly high. ***"He raises the poor from the dust and lift the needy from the ash hip"* Psalm 113:7.** The spirit of Lion of Judah makes you great. The spirit of Lion decorates you with garment of advertisement and knowledge. The Lord advertises you to fame. You see kindness and helpers.

The spirit of Lion makes you break out of the flesh and enter the chamber of life. The spirit of Lion of Judah builds and gives confidence when your rank changes and move from one level to another. You guide promotion with boldness and assurance. As you climb ladder of life, there are gate keepers. If you win a contract of 100 million dollars a prince will appear to you and ask how you make it. "How do you get to this level" if you can't answer, you will be cut off. But, if the spirit of the Lion of Judah dwell's in you, you will win. Do you think the poor widow of the Shunamite wasn't questioned? Everybody around knew she was a poor woman, suddenly she became rich as an oil magnate people come far and near to patronize.

The spirit of Lion of Judah opens the eyes. You may read the bible all over many times and never notice a particular verse. God will make you discover a verse and give deep meaning to it. The verse becomes part of you and personified of it. The spirit of Lion in you propagates the verse. Knowing the verse is applied and heaven answers. If the verse includes healing and you apply it in prayer, you get instant answer. There is power in the Word.

If you have capacity to build and intelligence to forge ahead, you need spirit of Lion to conquer and excel. This empowers you to prosper in anything you touch. The spirit X-tray's you in the studio of eternity to excel. The journey is from the valley to the mountain top. The spirit instructs you. You need encounter to be oracle of God.

It was capacity that Samuel had when under the tutelage of Eli. Samuel heard the voice; from experience Eli knew it was God's voice. He told Samuel, when you hear the voice again, say "Lord I hear you speak". Samuel developed in spirit and became a prophetic Lion everyone feared. Eli was

Samuel's instructor, the insurance policy that God put around men for encounter. The Bible says concerning Joshua, he was the servant of Moses. To Joshua, Moses laid hands on him, filling him with Spirit of wisdom to lead Israel. Elisha was referred to as a man that pours water in the hands of Elijah. You must be instructed in the phase of life. As instructor guides to accuracy, so is the spirit of Lion of Judah. In the multitude of counsel, there is safety.

It is the spirit of Lion of Judah that propels heavenly spirit to empower you to encounter spirit being. Spirits existed before creation. They were with God in heaven before Lucifer rebelled and fell. Since then, they became thorn in our flesh looking for how we would fall. This is why it is said, it is not about intelligence we live because they were before us and are quite intelligent. An excellent mind, a developed mind submitted to God is better than a mind which is not refined.

You are a victim if you are intelligent without God. Spirits are ancient being; they will outsmart you and cause your fall except spirit of Lion of Judah dwells in you. It is foolish to believe yours only. You can't be smarter than spirits. They have your biological history. They know your blood line and deficiency that operates there. The only way to conquer them is to link to the oldest among the spirit which is God. Every other sprit is created by another spirit. The spirit that creates is Elohim. When we connect to God we become older and advance than every other spirit. You will enter another technology, another gateway and gain wisdom that is not common among men. You will gain strategic advantage over Satan and the spirit.

There was darkness on earth for 400 years no prophet arises until a certain prophet. He started to do what is strange on earth; what has not happen before. He started to baptize men in the wilderness, in strange clothing. People were surprise but the spirit of Lion of Judah dwell in him. He was John the Baptist. I prophesy into your life, you will do strange things that will promote you in the Kingdom. The breakthrough that never happens in your linage, God will empower it to happen. Hope will never leave your family. The messiah that John the Baptist propagates appeared at last. John the Baptist fulfilled his mission on earth. Through encounter John's eyes open when he saw Jesus. The Lord shall open your spiritual eyes and antennal of encounter, in the name of Jesus. John the Baptist never read it in book that Jesus was coming for baptism, but confessed it. It is spirit of Lion of Judah in operation. He recognized Jesus without introduction. As he baptizes Jesus and rose of the water, heaven opened and a voice was heard, saying "This is my beloved son with whom I am well pleased". John the Baptist has discerning eyes because heavenly spirit dwells in him.

If you encounter the spirit in the supernatural realm spirit of Lion will envelope you. Dark spirit won't overcome you in the spirit or in the physical. They will try but shall fail. If you are empty in the spirit, you will be an easy prey. If Satan sees light around you, he will flee. The light is the work of the spirit of the Lion of Judah.

The spirit of Lion in Peter makes him recognize who was Jesus; as Christ the Son of God. Our Lord Jesus confirmed it. Peter said *"You are the Christ, the Son of the living God"* **Mathew 16:16.** Jesus confirmed his father in heaven revealed it to Peter. Revelation has source. The source is from the altar of God. The spirit of Lion of Judah of David linage to Jesus did it. That same hour, Peter was elevated to status of a Rock. Jesus said, *"And I tell you that you are Peter, and on this Rock I will build my church and the gates of Hades will not overcome it"*. **Mathew 16:18.** This is heavenly empowerment.

The spirit of Lion will enable you, handle all gates: the gates of liberty, the gates of revelation, the gate of problem and the gate of confusion and sorrow. If you are called the Lord will empower you to open gates that lead to success. If you are a candidate of the supernatural there are gates you will open before you excel. The book of **Psalm 24:7 says,** *"Lift up your heads O yea gates, be lifted up you ancient doors that the King can come in"*. What is your position? To be a Prophet, Pastor, Apostle, Teacher or Deacon doesn't mean you can open gates. You must be empowered and what empowers you is the Lion that dwells in you.

The spirit of Lion of Judah incubated Paul and Silas when they prayed and sang Hallelujah songs of deliverance to the Lord. There was sudden earthquake in the prison. The prison flung open and they were delivered. Gate will stand and will not let you enter if you are not filled with spirit that opens gates. If you don't address gate, your experience will waste, your credential will waste. You will be strangled. Paul and Silas will remain in prison until the gate open. Also, if chain fall off your hands and gate didn't open, you can't go out. If the gate is not open the King of glory will stay outside stranded. One strategy of advancement of life is to break the gate open. The battle you don't win will be a problem for you and your children. Locked gate will keep you in captivity.

The spirit of Lion of Judah breaks you out of the flesh and enters the chamber of supernatural. Many can't pray and stay with God, three, four or six hours. They are inconvenient and see it unhealthy. Those who are before the Lord are refreshed. No wonder David says I am happy when they say let's go to the house of God. The house of God is a fire power house that incubates and focuses the spirit to Zion. Your spirit is incubated with word of God, prayer, deliverance, healing and breakthrough. You are stabilized in God's presence until the light breaks out in the spirit realm. Prayer takes you to supernatural realm to have encounter with God. Life dwells where God dwells. Time of refreshing comes from the house of God. The spirit of Lion in you, makes you grow from strength to strength. No wonder the bible says, *"They will soar on wings like eagles, they will run and not grow weary, they will walk and not be faint"*. **Isaiah 40:31.**

The power of Lion of Judah is a download from heaven. You must have heavenly D.N.A. with God to have supernatural connection with heaven. Jesus never told us to pray about the mountain but to command the mountain. It is the spirit of Lion of Judah that will make you speak to the mountain and it will move. If you speak to a situation it will come to pass.

THE LION OF THE TRIBE OF JUDAH

PRAYER POINTS

1. Lion of Judah, thank you for protecting me, in the name of Jesus.
2. Lord Jesus, you are the Lion of the tribe of Judah, keep me fit every day by your power.
3. Lord Jesus, I come before you, forgive my sins by your power.
4. Blood of Jesus heal me within and strengthen me in the name of Jesus.
5. O Lord, give me spirit to live a holy life, in the name of Jesus.
6. Hands of God, part into two the Red Sea on my way to success in the name of Jesus.
7. Angel of God, put coal of fire in my tongue to do exploit in prayer and capacity building, in the name of Jesus.
8. I move from the valley to mountain top, in the name of Jesus.
9. Every idol of my father's house, troubling my soul, I pull you down in the name of Jesus.

10. Lord Jesus, empower me to triumph over temptation and sin in the name of Jesus.

11. O Lord, empower me to achieve extra-ordinary fits anywhere I go in the name of Jesus.

12. I carry spirit of Lion of Judah and destroy works of darkness in the name of Jesus.

13. Anointing of God, flow upon me in the name of Jesus.

14. Lion of Judah silence every contrary power that is against me and my God, in the name of Jesus.

15. Every serpentine spirit against me, your time is up, expire, in the name of Jesus.

16. O Lord, water the garden of my life for signs and wonders in the name of Jesus.

17. Dark scale in my face; remove by fire, in the order of Paul, in the name of Jesus.

18. O Lord, give me wisdom and bold spirit to handle every situation that comes my way, in the name of Jesus.

19. Every barrier along my way, clear away, in the name of Jesus.

20. Lord Jesus, let heaven trace good things to me, by your power.
21. Opportunities around me, locate me, in the name of Jesus.
22. Lord Jesus, give me strength to operate in the supernatural, in the name of Jesus.
23. Spirit of Adam and Eve in me that disobey God's command, come out of me, in the name of Jesus.
24. My weakness in prayer be defeated, in the name of Jesus.
25. Bread and wine shall not take Holy Spirit from me, in the name of Jesus.
26. I soar on wings like eagle and occupy height of glory, in the name of Jesus.
27. I shall not be defeated in the battle of life, in the name of Jesus.
28. O Lord, make me for greener pasture that swallows poverty in my linage, in the name of Jesus.

29. Satan get lost, Jesus is my Lord, in the name of Jesus.

30. Spirit of poverty, quit my life in the name of Jesus.

31. O Lord, enlarge my heart to welcome spirit of Lion of Judah.

32. Arrow of untimely death; backfire to the sender in the name of Jesus.

33. Doors of glory, doors of breakthrough begin to open to me in the name of Jesus.

34. Predators waiting for my downfall be terminated, in the name of Jesus.

35. Veil of darkness separating me from God, tear to pieces in the name of Jesus.

36. Voice of God, speak deliverance into my life, in the name of Jesus.

37. D.N.A. of Satan in my life be nullified, in the name of Jesus.

38. Satanic fire, heated to consume me, quench, in the name of Jesus.

39. Fourth man in my life; appear and rescue me in the name of Jesus.
40. Serpent that swallow my wealth, vomit it by fire, in the name of Jesus.
41. Every unfriendly friend that surround me, scatter in the name of Jesus.
42. Courage to conquer my enemy and excel in all I do, fill my heart, in the name of Jesus.
43. Wasters around me be wasted, in the name of Jesus.
44. Hands of God, release me from spirit Pharaoh that enslave me in the spirit in the name of Jesus.
45. Ladder of greatness, come alive and let me occupy great height, in the name of Jesus.
46. Lion of Judah, heal my foundation in the name of Jesus.
47. Spirit to pray and explore the earth and heaven, fall upon me, in the name of Jesus.

48. Lion of Judah remove pains and sorrow in my life that will make me deny God, in the name of Jesus.
49. Spirit of wickedness in my life, expire, in the name of Jesus.
50. Language of heaven blesses me, in the name of Jesus.

CHAPTER 2

WARFARE LIONS IN THE SCHOOL OF PRAYER

It is time the Lion in you awake in prayer. It is time your family arises in prayer and padlock the mouths of the enemy boasting you will not make it. It is time you pray and scatter wicked powers that gang up against you. It is time you receive anointing to exploit in the spirit and tap into the kingdom in the supernatural where spirits operate and heavens are downloaded. Be filled in the spirit like a Lion that roar for energy to conquer the jungle. John the Baptist added feather to his C.V. when he encountered Jesus in the Jordan. He was a prayer warrior who taught his disciples how to pray. Jesus disciples want to emulate him when they said to Jesus to teach them how to pray as John the Baptist taught his disciples. They want to roar like thunder in prayer as John the Baptist roar in prayer.

The words you pronounce either edify or sink you. Your words make you a giant or a dwarf in the spirit. Your words form prayers. You pray with understanding and speak with understanding. Spirit of Lion makes you encounter intimacy with God. Encounter reveals futility of Life. It is time to look at your maker and celebrate him for great things that will happen after this message. There is joy when a family, a tribe or a race is raised to bring joy to millions, and millions tap sources of greatness.

We were created in the order of God, so we must resemble him and take to his D.N.A. He is God of power; hence we must not be short changed by Satan. We must operate in the spirit more than a conqueror because our God is more than a conqueror. In marriage, office, calling or service we must be more than a conqueror. You have no excuse to live as a failure or defeated entity. You are created a champion.

God creates you in his image. He said, ***"Let us create man in our own image, in our likeness"***. **Genesis 1:26.** The word "our" is plural, meaning God the Father, God the Son, and God the Holy Spirit. The creation of man is unique because we pick all three in one. So we are created as all powerful in humanity, that is why we can invent and progress. We are intimidated by Satan, because God is our D.N.A. In you is the dimension of the Father, the Son and the Holy Ghost. When the Lion in you roar, you will perform more than expected. You can't be defeated; you have to be taught how to fail. Failure is not your portion neither is it in your D.N.A. People from the Lion of the tribe of Judah never fail. So, you will not fail. Failure is alien to you. It is natural for you to succeed.

Everybody have credential of him that is of the Lion of the tribe of Judah. It is your victory that reveals the Lion in you. In this message, you will begin to conquer, begin to dominate, and begin to win. It is not prerogatives of others but your inheritance.

As a Christian you are born with spirit of the Lion of the tribe of Judah, it is a function of D.N.A. The D.N.A of a winner is inside of you. This is what Adam missed when the serpent came to deceive him. He failed to realize, he had D.N.A of God at creation, so he fell for Satan and the story changed. As a man with D.N.A of God don't doubt in the order of Adam, go into prayer and conquer. The book of **1 John 4:4** says; ***"Ye are of God, little children, and have overcome them: because greater is he that is in you, than he that is in the world."*** We must not doubt our status any longer. You are a champion, enemy cannot defeat. Christ is in you, with hope of victory. Jesus is from the tribe of the Lion of Judah. You are in Christ with D.N.A of Christ. Your prayer is aroma to God.

Your dress, your artificial finger nails, your haircut, artificial lashes, the gold or chain in your neck, your shoe, or credential cannot defeat D.N.A of God. Everything submits to what God deposit in you. It is what abides in you that give you knowledge, wisdom and understanding. These are what energize the Lion in you to roar and clear way for you to prosper. Avoid what will not announce you in heaven. Avoid what will not make your journey in the spiritual realm smooth.

Jesus says, in my name cast out demons. It means you are with authority to do what Jesus does. You have his D.N.A. The Lion in Him is in you. What he does, you can do. Go into prayer until you occupy Gethsemane, where sweat is like blood. Where you glow and transfigured like Lion of the tribe of Judah. Your victory is tied to your association with Christ. It is God that is in you that give victory in addition to your certificate, helpers and knowledge. Your human development capacity is essential to glow God's anointing in you. You do exploits when loaded with the spirit of Lion of Judah. The tension of your prayer changes to open heavens for you to do exploit.

Your association is tied to Jesus Christ. If you hold to Christ in prayer, you will be a champion. As a champion, decide not to look at your weakness. The eyes of the Lord look to and fro for the weak to strengthen. What is weakness? It is when your spirit refuses to rise and fight battle. Look unto Jesus the author and finisher of our faith. Moses said I cannot speak. God answered who created the mouth? You are limiting God when you focus on your limitation. If you allow the Lion in you to rise, the weakness will bring glory to you. The Devil that plan to put you in captivity shall fail.

You are a Lion of the tribe of Judah. You have your D.N.A to Christ. A Lion in the jungle has his D.N.A. Bear doesn't come near Lion in the jungle. Lion walk cool with majesty. Lion doesn't fear. A

Lion that is a novice is a terror in the bush. All animals know; sheep know, antelopes know, bear knows, elephants know, all animals know this! Because of D.N.A the finger of a Lion is trained to tear, his teeth is built to tear. The resilience of a Lion is built for battle. There is something in the D.N.A of a Lion that makes it a killer. If Lion smell blood his elements are activated. Everyone born of God becomes a terror to kingdom of darkness. They are silenced with appearance of a Lion. You are of the Lion of the tribe of Judah loaded with light of God and anointing of the heavenly.

You are a Lion of the tribe of Judah. Beware of this! What you think you don't have is inside of you. What you are looking for are already in your inside; you are not just aware. How can you be like Christ and be demonized. How can you be like Christ and be poor? How can you be like Christ and be sick? Brethren, do you not know when

Jesus came he took everything away. He took your curse away. He took your sin away. He took your shortcomings away. Sin is the basis of your fall. He took it away. Your D.N.A improves the spirit of Lion in you. Christ is our hope of glory and champion of our cause. How can you ever be defeated when his D.N.A possess you?

The Lion comes majestically in the jungle. It is never in a hurry. The Lion has gravity like a king. Lion is conscious of its D.N.A. When a man with spirit of Lion steps out there is a way he dresses. You don't see him dress naked. He is noble. He never talk carelessly. He is a warrior, more than a conqueror. These are your characteristics. You are a sign and wonder to your generation.

You are not alone; the hair of your head is not counted but numbered. *"But even the very hairs of your head are all numbered. Fear not therefore: ye are of more value than many sparrows."* **Luke 12:7.** This means you are important before God. He won't like you defeated in the battle of life. You are a Lion in the battle of life. You won't be defeated by powers of darkness, but grow strength to strength. Your strength is a function of your presence before God in the spirit. This is what makes you a Lion in your vicinity, in office, in your father's house and everywhere you go.

The spirit of Lion gives ability to see the future, and tap the present to fulfill the future. The Lord told Abraham, the far your eyes can see I give unto you. Abraham believed and builds faith to fulfill it through his generational children that eventually occupied the Promised Land. This is not ordinary. It is the spirit of Lion that flowed in his vein through generations.

You pray to have knowledge of what you possess. Your knowledge is your possession. The extent of your knowledge is the boundary of your possession. Let the Lion in you have knowledge of what you pray about. The Devil won't fold hands, he will like to corrupt what you see and hear to distract and frustrate you. If Devil gets to your soul, he corrupts your inheritance.

Our work on earth is largely warfare. The Devil doesn't want anyone to succeed over the power of darkness. The earth is darkness according to **Isaiah 60:2.** *"See, darkness covers the earth and thick darkness is over the people, but the Lord rises upon you and his glory appear over you"*. Anywhere you are on earth is darkness. The presence of darkness cannot take over your life if you are surrounded by light. The excellence of light is; the light shines in darkness and the darkness apprehend it not. Your prayer illuminates light to conquer darkness. It is the spirit of Lion in you that lights you and the environment. You will shine as prayer warrior and possess your possession. You see into the future with ability to shape the future. To see what you want, to have what you want and have all available in Christ.

Where you are today is what you saw yesterday and what you said yesterday. Nobody made today available for you; you create today what you see and by what you are. What you will be tomorrow is a product of saying what you are seeing now and what you are saying now. You must guide your utterances and the steps you take is important. You must grow in spirit, pray in spirit and download from the supernatural as a Lion of the tribe of Judah. If you are not careful, Satan will corrupt your mind from fulfilling your destiny. It is good to fulfill the future you desire.

There is what intervention of God is. The Lord did it when Samuel erected an altar of God and pours oil on it and called it Ebenezer. As from that day, the hands of God were against the Philistines **1 Samuel 7:12**. Prayer altar needs oil of victory and oil of breakthrough. It needs oil of favor and mercy to explode in the spirit like a Lion that destroys enemy. You need intervention because there are errors in the past. If you build correctly there would be insurance on it and there won't be need for intervention. Since, we are not perfect, we pray for intervention of God. As a Christian you must minimize error to get to destination of life safely and better.

Brethren, arise, let God introduce economy of life in your spirit to transfigure and make you glow. Your spirit glows as you make contact with God. The light in your life determines your glory in the Lord. When you attend church activity the glory you carry increases. The glory that comes upon you will give authority to walk through life because glory is a force in the spirit. This is why the more glorify a man has, the more dominion he commands. Circumstance will begin to obey you because you possess the spirit of Lion of Judah.

The spirit of Lion in you awakes if you improve or work on your spirit. You need transformation of soul because what you become is a record on your soul. Sin, infirmity and affliction are record or writings on your soul. Fear is writing on your soul. Everything that forms your personality is a document that your soul keeps. When you go for service one of the many things that happen to your soul is that light comes to your soul and record of death is deleted. Your soul is liberated from fear. Your soul is liberated from sin. Your soul is liberated from iniquity. All that reduces potency of your soul is deleted. This is the situation that quickens lion of Judah in you into action. You must be liberated. The Lion in you must arise and do the unthinkable to the enemy of your soul.

It is important the soul is healed. The souls of many are in captivity. Many souls are bruised, tortured and helpless. There are many that are weak and depressed. They can't find energy to fulfill their destiny. They know what to do but are fired. They know they should read, but they can't read. This is soul sickness. When the soul is sick heaven may not respond. The succor is, when you are in church service your soul begins to radiate positive to healing. Your power begins to increase and thought towards life increases. As your soul improves it affects your environment.

Changes first happen within before it happens in external. The spirit controls the physical. Your internal emotion and character is directly proportional to your natural realm. If the internal is affected it will manifest in the external. To explode the activity of Lion in your soul, pray for heavenly light to function within for sound healing.

Warfare Lions shouldn't be blind in the spirit. If you build right utterance it will build the future you desire. Devil can't compromise such future. Seeing in the natural is continuous, as you grow your eyes will open. Seeing in the spirit is not automatic. There are things you do to see in the spirit. Many are blind in the sprit because they don't know what to do to quicken their sight in the spirit. If your vision is not pure, God will not put his validation upon it.

Arouse your spirit to capture your environment like a wounded Lion. The moment your understanding begins to change, your experience will change. Devil cannot stop your manifestation if you have requisite understanding. The reason the Devil appears very strong is because our ignorance empowers him. The moment our ignorance is removed, the helplessness of the Devil is made manifest. No demon can affect you if you have the right understanding.

From time of creation there is abundance of our needs. We are created to dominate; for example, when God created Adam and Eve, God created enough land, oxygen and mineral resources. God didn't create more, as population increases. The oxygen two people use on the day of creation is what billions use today. It is an opportunity for the lion in you to dominate and secure the future that will announce your star. God brings us into abundance. It is your fault if you are not accessing it. Create space to reach God, and God to access you.

Prayer warrior are determined and focused. They pray against distraction and follow principle of spiritual discipline. In the spirit, looking forward is foresight, looking backward is retrogression, looking sideways is distraction. It is not about seeing; it is about seeing the right direction. And the only way you can see the right direction is to seek God's will for your life. Lions don't flock with other animals in the jungle. Know what you do and how you do it. Don't be a copycat. We call them follow, follow. What they pursue may not be what God has in stock for you. If people are in the wrong direction and you are a copycat, you will find yourself in a deep pit. If you are in the wrong direction speed is not an advantage. If God calls you to serve him but go into politics, you will end up in penury, end up in frustration and weak. Your failure will be a dislocation.

A prayer warrior in Christ must concentrate in prayer and will of God. Since your neck rotates you will see things you don't like. Develop eyes of discipline that cannot be corrupted. Develop mind that cannot be corrupted with sideway attractions. You will see half naked girls and women. Don't be carried away. They will destroy your calling and makes you candidate of the Hades. Those who sojourn such ways don't return save. They are casualty of life. *"None who go to her return or attain the paths of life."* **Proverbs 2:19.** You may end up not fulfilling your destiny. But if the Lion in you roar in prayer you will escape the hardline of Satan.

Avoid anxiety in life. It is now common among Nigerians and other Africans to move to Europe, America and Asian countries. The anxiety is so much that some resigned from work and travel with family, only to get there and see they made mistake. When they get job, they pay tax which they avoid at home. Since their children are not citizens, they pay exorbitant school fees. Accommodation and utility swallow their take home pay. Feeding is high, at the end of the day they are cockroach before Lion! They regret their action.

Their attitude resembles that of Lot who pick flourishing forest good for herder and farming. Before he realized it, he found himself in Sodom and Gomorrah, a land that swallow destiny. Not all that glitter is Gold. Africans have the habit of worshiping money. They die in penury in the spirit because the manner the wealth is accumulated is questionable. Their Lion die and may find it difficult to walk through the narrow way to heaven. Let the Lion in you wake so that you don't walk into Sodom waiting to destroy you because of your appetite. When men cannot discern in life their appetite is God.

In every step you take let love operate. Love is a weapon that attracts development. No matter how prayerful you are, without love is cracks that reduce destiny to nothing. Always open doors of love to people around you. You are in cage when you think yourself and forget others. God did not create you to be selfish. The little help you can render do it. This is how the Lion in you will have strength. This doesn't mean you should be a Father Christmas, spending lavishly or giving out money anyhow. If people realize it, they will bombard you like swarm of bees and suck you dry. The little you can do, do it. Your thinking should not be around you and your family alone! When God calls you out of your body you become naked because of your appetite.

Many are not working in the victory available to them because they are not aware. Beware of the spirit that dwells in you. Avoid gossip and be occupied with the spirit of the Lion in you. Do you ever hear Jesus gossip or mock? He is occupied all the time. Involve in prayer, involve in studying the word, involve in good sleep, not mockery. Lions don't have time to gossip. Emulate Jesus; use your mouth like his. He speaks and the blind see. He speaks and the deaf hear. He speaks and the disease vanished. Pattern your life after him and when you do, everything around you will change. Your prayer life changes as well.

Emulate Jesus to do more than the prophet of the old. In his name, nothing shall be impossible. If you believe and you have faith wonders will wrought in your hands. Moses led four million through the Red Sea after he raised his rod to part it into two. Elijah strikes Jordan, it part for him to pass. These are waters. But Jesus walked on water. It is called dominion; he doesn't need to part it. It is one level to part the sea; it is another level to walk on the water. Jesus action is a realm superior to nature. It is a realm superior to limitation. When God give us the D.N.A of Jesus, He gives us the best. You are in the territory of wonders and miracles. Awake the Lion in you to have scores of victory Satan cannot comprehend. Jesus gives us all things, meaning you should not doubt. Let your life end on the cross and the life you live now begin on the resurrection. Resurrect now and do wonders with the D.N.A you have in Christ. Look like Christ, strife for Christ. Arise, let your D.N.A arise. You must pray and win the battle.

Your parents may be great, it is good. Your uncles may be great, it is good. No one is greater than Jesus. Your parents or uncles will have one obstacle or another as they journey in life. There is only one person that was unstoppable when he came to this world; that is, Jesus. Even death couldn't hold him down. He triumphed over death. Look like Jesus that conquered death. Look like Jesus, it is a name everybody is exploring. Explore him so that your destiny may change. Explore him so that you breakthrough. Explore him to do wonders in life. Explore him to be a prayer champion.

To be a lion of the tribe of Judah, be conscious of the D.N.A of God in your life. Whosoever does the will of God over cometh the world. The world means nothing if you do his will. Other things fall in place if you do his. The Bible says, seek heaven first other things will follow. It won't profit you to gain the world and lose heaven. Avoid rat race for visa, rat race to build or have a car or cars. I do not say, don't have any of these but don't pursue it in a do or die manner. Everything will fall in place when it is time. Pray, so that it comes when due.

Awake the Lion in you into prayer to conquer and win. Christ in you can give you a car. Christ in you can give you a visa. Christ in you can give you buildings.

The spirit of Lion promotes light of God. As a man or woman in Christ you are a light carrier. Light of God makes you walk over valley of death unhurt. Light of God match and destroy serpents and scorpions. It opens closed doors hidden to you by powers of darkness. Helpers are located, identified and embraced for great exploits. If you don't have light you are finished because the lion in you will sleep and be weak. The book of Psalm says, *"Have respect unto the covenant: for the dark place of the earth are full of the habitations of cruelty"*. **Psalm 74:20.** According to **Isaiah 60:2,** darkness shall cover the whole earth. *"For, behold, darkness shall cover the earth, and gross darkness the people: but the Lord shall arise upon thee, and his glory shall be seen upon* *thee"*. Darkness is evil. It rises to kill and destroy men. Jesus is the light that intimidates and silence darkness. Arise in prayer; let the light in you shine over darkness to arouse spirit of Lion in you. Darkness was not created to have authority over light. *"And the light shineth in darkness; and the darkness comprehended it not."* **John 1:5.** The result you command is the outcome of light you possess. The moment there is light result becomes by product. When the Devil wants to attack you, he comes for the light you carry. The light God gives you become the source of your victory, hold it tight, guide it well, let it occupy and shine in you. Light is the word of God. *"In him was life, and that life was the light of all mankind".* **John 1:4.** Your insurance in this kingdom is the light at your disposal. Light is a commander; allow it in your life so that you may shine. Light confess authority. Light confess power. When you carry light, you carry dominion.

Most Christians live carelessly. They don't control their mouth. They eat anyhow and everywhere. They sleep about as unguided animals. They visit places without direction. How can the giant in them survive? How can Holy Spirit fortify them with protection? Why will they not fall? The spirit of Lion in them will walk out of them. From your talk, to what you do or eat affects your spirit being. If you want to be a Lion in the spirit, you must be governed by law. To achieve it, you must be a discipline child of God. Job says, I have a covenant with my eyes against lust. ***"I made a covenant with my eyes not to look lustfully at a young woman."* Job 31:1.** He has consecration for purity. The book of proverbs warned against lust. It says there are things that seem good to the eyes, but when you embark on it, it leads to death. You build your life into consecration.

The Lion in you can be abused before birth. Thank your mother who consecrates her life for you to exist and excel in life. The mother of Samson was warned against strong wine. This is consecration. Wine would have swallowed the strength and covenant for Samson, unfortunately, Samson undo himself. He did not consecrate himself to Israel's linage but ended up in the camp of enemy. Championship is born from the womb of consecration.

Opposite was Joseph to Samson. Joseph consecrated himself. He never fell to lust. He said how can I do this and offend God, when Potiphar wife wanted him to sleep with her. *"No one is greater in this house than I am. My master has withheld nothing from me except you, because you are his wife. How then could I do such a wicked thing and sin against God?"* **Genesis 39:9.** The spirit of Lion in Joseph saved him from lust that would have buried his destiny. He walked from prison to palace because he consecrated himself.

Daniel was a lion himself. His story touched the heart. He was a prisoner of conscience because he was one among thousands captured and taken to Babylon. Babylon which should be a place of captivity became a place of liberty. The Lion in him arose in a foreign land. No one knew Daniel in Israel but Babylon. Circumstances that swallow destiny popularized him. He prayed until he was cast into den of lions. He came out save and his popularity explodes. This is act of discipline and concentration.

What of Meshach, Sheldrake and Abednego? They refused to bow down and worship Babylonian idol. They overcame pressure. They stood by their point. They refused to be brainwashed. They stick to their gun. They were fearless. They allow the spirit of Lion in them take credit of the day. They were thrown into the fire. They did not shout for help. In the fire awaits them the fourth man. They clap and dance in the fire. The heat of the fire turned to air-condition. They felt good in the fire. They won the day! The spirit of Lion of Judah in them won the day.

Daniel grew from one authority to another. There was a time the king dreamt and no one could interpret it. All the wise men in Babylon gathered before the king but could not do anything. Daniel came to the scene. He knew and interpreted the handwriting. So, when you are in doubts call Daniel to answer your need. He understands beyond measure. Daniel never follow trend of life but heaven.

Prayer champions are not carried away by worldly trends. They refuse to follow vogue. This is what reigns now. It is not in their dictionary. They dress modest, cut their hair modest, eat modest and walk modest. They are not the party type. They don't eat about. They are radical and hungry to study the Word and pray. They fast and pray. There hunger is prayer. They seek knowledge, wisdom and understanding. They seek avenue for development. They know the rule; if you don't work you don't eat. So they are not lazy. They don't believe in lies. They are not the commercial or contract pastors. These are not people that don't see vision but tells lies. They are Lions in the house of God while others are hawks and the wicked in sheep clothing.

Therefore, focus Christ and let your lion rise. Don't be manipulated by energy of the society. How can you mentor a system and want to change the system. Are you not deceiving yourself? You must be consecrated from the system to exercise dominion over it. You must have consecrated over the system. You must have consecrated around your mouth, in your marriage, in your eyes, in your studies and among friends. There is a level consecration bring in makes you live in the supernatural. Great men and women are rigid. They are busy, reason fast and not found wanting in development. This is what a man or woman of prayer does.

Satan knows where he goes. He knows you are a potential danger if you are the prayerful type. This is the reason your prayer is first attacked before you are attacked. If he can't do it, he concludes you are dangerously dangerous to his kingdom. Satan's intention is; you go to club, drink and smoke, run after opposite sex and doomed. Discipline yourself it is not every number you save in your phone. Don't spend hours on your phone. Time waits for nobody. Discuss what will improve you and avoid careless talks. People guided by spirit of lion hardly waste opportunities; hardly play about and hardly play around. They focus on opportunities, they invest in great ideas. They save the number of people that have roles to play in their destiny. Be a prayer warrior.

When a champion pray he does not look lukewarm in the altar. He is wild in the spirit and aggressive against the enemy in the supernatural. He prays like a man loaded with spirit of lion. He is fervent and dangerous in the spirit. He is focus in prayer. He is smart in prayer. He doesn't say vain things. He is bold like a lion. He prays with vision. He prays fervent prayer. There is a way devil will see you before he attacks you. It is effectual fervent prayer that shakes kingdom of darkness. Effectual speaks of focus, fervent speaks of intensity.

When champion pray there is intensity, when he is dressing up there is intensity. There is urgency about his life. He believes in, ***"I must work the works of him that sent me, while it is day: the night cometh, when no man can work." John 9:4.*** You don't have all the time. The time is too short. It is as if 24 hours a day is small. You must be focus, diligent and organize in what you do. These are articles of intensity. He knows what to do, when to do and how to do it and energy to do it.

He doesn't drag his feet when action is needed. He takes time to do things in a perfect way. Don't waste time, some people wasted 10 years of there life because of five minutes lateness. You were told, arrive 9:00 O'clock and you came five minutes after 9:00 0'clock. The gate was locked and you weren't answered. You lost it! There was no spirit of Lion of Judah operating in you.

What God wants to do you miss it because of five minutes. You can't be lukewarm and lackadaisical and make it in life. Don't use prophecy to cover up where there should be discipline. They use impartation to cover up where they should put diligence. If all bishops in your country lay hands on you, and you are not prayerful, discipline, energetic and focus you will fail! If you use human connection to cover up where there should be competence, you will lose. Special warning! Special warning! Don't say you want to help someone because he is a Christian, find out his capacity.

Avoid procrastination in the journey of life. What you should do at 24 years you are for it at 40 years old. You are beginning to reap failure. You will put all effort in place before you can succeed. You don't wait for tomorrow what you can do today, because tomorrow has its problem. Great men and women finish the work that is meant for today, today and sometimes they bring tomorrow's work into today. For taking today's work into tomorrow they prefer doing next tomorrow work into today. They finish and finish on time. Awake your heart! Awake your mind! Awake your energy! Awake your prayer life! Be a man or woman that has the spirit of Lion of Judah. The time is now! Awake to your rising!

What made many fail is arrogance. They are arrogant to the extent of looking down on everyone around them. They are proud to potential helpers.

They lose opportunity that comes their way. Who do you resemble with arrogance? Note this! Jesus the son of God needed John the Baptist to announce him. As he rises out of Jordan River, heaven opens and declare. ***"And lo a voice from heaven, saying, This is my beloved Son, in whom I am well pleased."* Matthew 3:17**. John the Baptist was the architect of Jesus announcement to the world before he started his ministry. You are finish, if you don't know how to access help. Jesus carried the position of humility. Spirit of humility provokes help more than utterance. When a man is humble, even God helps him. God hates arrogance. If you don't humble, you go nowhere. Those not humble burn the bridges they will take in their life time. If a relationship is to fail have it on record you do your best. God raise men to make men. Jesus needed John to create a season for him. Even Elisha needed Elijah, Moses needed Joshua, and Paul needed Ananias.

Brethren, let your spirit boil for change. Let the boiling water be truthfulness. Nothing burns a bridge like lies. Lies distance you from helpers. Confidence is eroded. No one likes to associate with you. They believe they are not safe. The character of liars stands against them. Lies destroy goodwill. Lies distance you from God. There is easy access on the platform of truthfulness. When you err say you err. When you lie, quickly correct it. Don't let it be discovered later that what you said was a lie, because the hardest thing to regain is trust. Let the lion in you vomit truth. It is a power that produces good result.

It takes diligence to give power to one who has love. A man without love frustrates who comes his way. He is a sadist, selfish, wicked, tribal, racist and not accommodative. God loves those who love more. Jesus said, when I was hungry you give me food, when I was in prison you take care of me. Love builds, it never pull down. Until God finds love he doesn't empower. Until God see the spirit of lion in you to go far and love others, your prayer may not go far. There are people who pray and have it in mind that if they are blessed they won't help certain people they regard as enemy. Stop it! Your lion will not fly high!

PRAYER POINTS

1. O Lord, I thank you for the spirit of warrior deposited in my heart, in the name of Jesus.
2. My soul be liberated from sin and receive forgiveness in the name of Jesus.
3. O heaven, hearken to my prayer, in the name of Jesus.
4. Holy Spirit, guide me to pray with focus and get advantage over my enemy in the name of Jesus.
5. Holy Spirit, guide me, enemy of my soul disappear by fire, in the name of Jesus.

6. Spirit of fear in me, disappear by fire, in the name of Jesus.
7. Satanic territorial powers bow and scatter, in the name of Jesus.
8. Lord Jesus, give me appetite to pray, in the name of Jesus.
9. O Lord, give me spirit to encounter Jesus.
10. Light of God; expel darkness troubling me in the spirit in the name of Jesus.
11. My yesterday and today shall not consume my future, in the name of Jesus.
12. Cup of disgrace, cup of sorrow, cup of failure and debt designed for me break, in the name of Jesus.
13. Heavenly insurance, insure my breakthrough and success in the name of Jesus.
14. O Lord, empower me with authority to silence Satan, in the name of Jesus.
15. Power to study the Word; incubate me by fire, in the name of Jesus.

16. Spirit of infirmity and affliction causing tears in my life, expire in the name of Jesus.

17. I am unstoppable by Satan, in the name of Jesus.

18. Serpent and Scorpions assign against me, die, in the name of Jesus.

19. My soul shall not be corrupted by Satan or bow to the devil, in the name of Jesus.

20. Every embargo placed upon my spirituality, I pull you down, in the name of Jesus.

21. Every dark covenant against my prayer life, break, in the name of Jesus.

22. Yokes troubling my prayer and my foundation break in the name of Jesus.

23. Satanic investments against my destiny to prosper catch fire and burn to ashes in the name of Jesus.

24. Arrow of frustration fired against me backfire, in the name of Jesus.

25. Glory killers assign to suffocate my joy, today is your last day, expire, in the name of Jesus.

26. Satanic seeds in my foundation wither, in the name of Jesus.

27. Every power of Herod tracing my star, expire, in the name of Jesus.

28. Spirit of Goliath assigned to padlock my mouth be terminated in the name of Jesus.

29. Poison diluting my prayer, dry up, in the name of Jesus.

30. Evil birds flying around to pick my prayer and swallow it fall down and die, in the name of Jesus.

31. Powers working against my destiny scatter, in the name of Jesus.

32. Evil sleep troubling my prayer life comes to end today in the name of Jesus.

33. Lion of Judah in me roar against enemies in my family, in my office, in my marriage and environment in the name of Jesus.

34. Knowledge and wisdom from above incubate me, in the name of Jesus.

35. My prayer life, receive supernatural oxygen to prosper and conquer in the name of Jesus.
36. Satanic plantations design to trouble my future expire, in the name of Jesus.
37. O Lord, give me energy to fulfill my destiny, in the name of Jesus.
38. Every opportunity around me favors me by fire, in the name of Jesus.
39. I bind the evil power of strongman molesting me, in the name of Jesus.
40. Fresh favor of God; pursue me, locate me and bless me, in the name of Jesus.
41. I am a prayer champion, not a prayer failure, in the name of Jesus.
42. O God arises; break the alliance of the enemy against my prosperity, in the name of Jesus.
43. My generation shall know peace in the name of Jesus.
44. The far my eyes could see, the more my breakthrough shall be, in the name of Jesus.

45. Battles and warfare shall not consume me, in the name of Jesus.
46. After prayer, I shall celebrate in the name of Jesus.
47. O Lord, purge my life of impurity in the name of Jesus.
48. My prayer shall not be in bondage, in the name of Jesus.
49. I will not be defeated in the battle of life, in the name of Jesus.
50. My prayers restore my rights and privileges to me in the name of Jesus.
51. Agent of darkness attacking my prayer life expires, in the name of Jesus.
52. My prayers become pillars of greatness and breakthroughs in my house in the name of Jesus.
53. Life-lifting power, locate me in the name of Jesus.
54. Enemy shall not waste my life, shall not waste my opportunity in the name of Jesus.

CHAPTER 3

THE WARRIORS OF CHRIST IN HEAVEN

Spread your net into the world in prayer to drag everyone into the house of God, for eventual travel to Zion. You do this in prayer and evangelism. Many are perishing out there. Some are confuse. Some are lonely and depressed. Some are aware of Christ but couldn't make move, else, they are killed for embarrassing Christ. It is when you apply the Spirit of Lion you apply heaven's voice to them before answer can be got.

What happens in the spirit realm is massive, big and enormous. There are depths of sacrifices we must make. There are certain things God cannot commit to you if you are a liar, if you are still a fornicator. We know God has forgiven you but experientially you must stay clear of it if God should commit good things to your hands.

Irresponsible Christian cannot be tolerated at this time.

The plan of the devil is to keep believers of the world in bondage. The devil is at work to stop us entrance into our ordination. There have been many dead Lions; there have been many sleeping warriors in the hands of Satan. It is time to wake up. There are encroachments around your borders. There are infiltrations and suffocation of destiny in the spirit.

Are you awake as patriarch of the old? The church alone cannot do it all. Men of valor must be involved. Daniel was a good example. He went on his knee and prayed to God. He prayed until he got answer. The Lion in him was not weak.

Arise as missionaries of the old, minister of the old that understand the language that set destiny free. Ready to take the kingdom to the end and advance the territory of the kingdom even lives and threatened. To receive message in churches and go home is not enough. Who will take the message to arise Afghanistan, India, and Pakistan? Men must rise! Women must rise! Children must rise as well!

Intercessors must wake up. Prayer warriors must wake up. Teachers, Apostles and Pastors must wake up. The Lion in them must not sleep. They must know the work ahead. There shouldn't be room for laziness. Energy must be appropriated to the movement. They must commit themselves to it even if there is nothing to eat and drink. If we continue building houses at the expense of praying and raising warrior, Christianity will be swept under the carpet. To build is good, but it shouldn't be at the expense of Christ kingdom. Our men will prefer to leave in caves instead of the house they build because there will be more security in the house they build than in Christ kingdom. This is why we should wake up, intercessor must rise. The lion in you must rise.

There is a place you enter in the spirit where lust will die. There is a place you enter in the spirit where trust is imparted like injection. There is a place you enter in the spirit where faith is impacted. There is a place you enter in the spirit where wisdom is granted. Paul grew in the spirit and acquired wisdom. He said the gospel I preach was not taught of any man, I received it from the Lord. So there is a place you enter where you receive massage for your generation. May God raise generation that is ready to pray. Half of the job is done.

Prayer is important so that we don't build for children of bond woman to occupy. There were times they boast the churches we build belong to them. They mean it. They will tell you, and boast the land you buy and the buildings are for us in years to come. It is a challenge if kingdom children are not raised. We are always after what God will give. We never think how we advance our land in the spirit. God provides everything we need in the beginning. He created Adam and provided all for him. The business of God is beyond what you need. He was in the garden where he lacks nothing. So if what you come to God for is your need, then you have not seen a bigger picture, there is a kingdom to advance. Why do God come to Adam in the cool of the day and do it every day? There is a kingdom to advance. To advance the kingdom, the spirit of lion of Judah have role to play.

What is the weight of Adam's fellowship with God? His fellowship did not hold water. He lost to the serpent. To bridge the gap, prayer came to be. The communication gap reduced. If you can't pray now you can't contribute to kingdom advancement. We have to pray until the element of this world end. God can only commit to us if only we prepared a premise for him through prayer.

This is the reason the bible says in **Isaiah 40:28-31:** *"Have you not known? Have you not heard?, the everlasting God, the LORD, the Creator of the ends of the earth, neither faints nor is weary. His understanding is unsearchable. He gives power to the weak, and to those who have no might He increases strength. Even the youths shall faint and be weary, and the young men shall utterly fall, but those who wait on the LORD shall renew their strength; they shall mount up with wings like eagles, they shall run and not be weary, they shall walk and not faint."*

God did not promise them wine but wings to soar high. There they mingle with divinity. They become an extension of the supernatural being. Those that mount up wings and operate in the divinity are better and exposed to man that has a million in his account. Why? The man in the supernatural realm can co-ordinate in prayer; command in prayer, rebuke in prayer and excel in prayer. If the Lion in him triggers and accomplish breakthrough in the spirit he excels. The spirit controls the physical. Don't joke with prayer. It is your battle axe. Those that embrace economy of prayer fear not, they excel.

You become institution in this realm no one can harass. You are host of God no one can touch. It is not quoting the scripture but waking early to enter the realm in prayer. Wake at night to wrestle and soar high in the heavens to conquer and maintain territory. You can't have impact until you host God to the degree of how you handle your situation. Prayer makes your soul host God. As you pray, you build hunger for more and makes you an astronaut in the spirit realm. The Lord will create intimacy with you and show you patterns of what to be. The heaven open with new ideas and discovery. All these are product of spiritual download.

People don't wake up one day and prefer to dress naked, it is spiritual download. There is territorial energy level that convinces him or her to dress that way. There is territorial evil picture showed her and accepted in his/her heart. There is territorial energy level that regulates her choice. It is not ordinary. Before you know it, he lost his radar on earth. He lost focus and strength to pray. He does not have capacity to resist. Is he a Christian? Yes, but he doesn't understand the technology of download. Men that transverse and hook to heaven cannot be flooded one side. A woman that dresses half naked cannot pull him down. God quickens his hunger and appetite for prayer. Their appetites have been fortified by the volume of spiritual work they download. They are the type worldly songs are not moved. There ears are blocked to such songs because of download from the supernatural.

You can't overcome naked dress with discipline. What you need is saturation. What you need is alignment with heavenly. You can't overcome it based on carefulness. What you need is download. You must be prayerful and ascend to heaven. If you open Facebook they are there. If you open Instagram they are there. If you go to the market they are there. If you go to airport they are there in there madness. If you go to lecture room they are there. In campus they are there. Every day we have photograph coming from hades in the form of ladies and men. You better pray so that prayer will become aroma around you to chase them away. They are dark agents. If you greet them you are in trouble. If they greet you, you are in trouble. You must develop thick skin and be host of God. You must tarry like Peter and the Apostle in prayer to awaken your heart and make spirit of lion in you take control.

The reason you are struggling with what you are struggling with is because the download is not yet complete. There are measures you need to download that regulate your choice. Download is a capacity you can't resist if you are in the supernatural realm. You can't understand the technology of download. You need to be saturated with God. You need to be saturated with energy of the invisible. A lady was modest for 17 years before admission. When she came in, she now realizes her cloth doesn't match campus dress. Three months later, she changed. She starts dressing naked. The same year she was deflowered. Why? She couldn't travel far in prayer. She lost the lion of virginity in her. She could not download. She did not have the capacity to resist. She doesn't understand the technology of prayer.

If you go to men saturated in prayer, naked dress can't move them. The reason is, they are fortified with the volume of supernatural power. There are people things don't move. Everything in the physical is a product of download. There are princes in darkness that download wrongs into your life. That is why your character changes and couldn't control your appetite for the world. Men and women that download the heavenly are not moved of worldly songs. They entered the spirit of download and tap from it.

Emulate giants that download in the bible. Paul is a good example of men that know God. He has the capacity to download. His appetite has been fortified by the volume of what he downloaded. He downloads too much. His words are conviction. Christians of that time are downloaders. They are spiritually strong. What they say travel far in the spirit. When next you see them, they are loaded. You can't tell lies before them because they are downloaders.

Jacob told his children sit around me and let me tell you what will before you in the future. He knew the future because of download. He rebuked Reuben, for defiling his bed with one of his wives.

Reuben never made it as the first born of the family. This is the effect of negative download. Reuben who supposed to be a man of wisdom and excellence did not prosper. Do you know why? It is because of negative download. Men with download can change your destiny. We can't change our word until we download God into our spirit and heaven back it up. In **Hebrew 11:32** it is written: *"And what shall I more say? for the time would fail me to tell of Gideon, and of Barak, and of Samson, and of Jephthae; of David also, and Samuel, and of the prophets"* The name of Samuel was mentioned as a warrior, one who conquered territory. It was not Samuel that fought it is angel. This is power of download. He was with God in the spirit. When you walk, angels are with you doing things you are not even aware. When David rebuked Mount Gilboa, which did not rise up to fight the death of Jonathan and Saul is download. Who told him the mount contributed to his death? It is alignment with heaven.

Joshua said, let the sun stand still and let the moon stopped. it came to pass. This is downloading from heaven. This is the account.

¹² Then spake Joshua to the LORD in the day when the LORD delivered up the Amorites before the children of Israel, and he said in the sight of Israel, Sun, stand thou still upon Gibeon; and thou, Moon, in the valley of Ajalon.

¹³ And the sun stood still, and the moon stayed, until the people had avenged themselves upon their enemies. Is not this written in the book of Jasher? So the sun stood still in the midst of heaven, and hasted not to go down about a whole day. Joshua 10:12-13.

The sun did not make haste to go down. We need men that can host heaven and host God.

We have too many Pastors that can change circumstance. But are they ready? We have too many prophets, teachers, apostles and evangelist that cannot saturate the heaven or click the invisible. They can't download because they are of the world. Equip yourself with download. Saturate the supernatural. Let the spirit of Lion in you arise and download God.

Let your voice break network of demons and powers of darkness, so that you network and prevail. If the number of your friends on earth are more than the number of your friends in the spirit you are weak. David said in **Psalm 18:29**: *"For by thee I have run through a troop; and by my God have I leaped over a wall."* Can only David do this? There is a spiritual networking that gives David special help. Look at John the Baptist only him in the wilderness, eating wild honey bees with Girdle belt. He communicates with angels. There is spiritual networking happening. This is Spiritual network in operation. He cried repent, repent for the kingdom of God is at hand. What does it take to say repent in public if it is not spiritual? He knew what is at stake. John the Baptist knew it is spiritual. He came in the spirit of Elijah and needed to stay in the wilderness. He needs angelic support. Fear must not occupy his heart. He needs networking with the spirit in heaven. He needs to download. He needs spiritual download and spiritual anointing.

The anointing of Elijah changed his culture. The anointing changed his dress code. The anointing changed his language. He applies anointing of heaven. You can do it as well. Network your prayer with heaven and do what should be done. It is supernatural networking. You will migrate to a higher level with innumerable angels where justice is perfected. Some of us need to connect with Elijah. Some of us need to connect with Jeremiah. Some of us need to connect with David. Some of us need to connect with Paul. Some of us need to connect with Peter. It is supernatural networking. When some pastors preach they are taken to heaven to witness the situation. What they say and how he preaches will be different because of supernatural networking. Our advantage is on the mountain of mount Zion and you must find your level there.

When it is time for John to write the book of Revelation, something strange happened. The same John wrote the book of John, he wrote 1st John, 2nd John, 3rd John, when it was time to write the book of Revelation he was told you can't write this on earth. So he was taken up to a different level. He was taken to heaven. He was carried to heaven from earth and was taken to heaven. He was taken to the beginning of time; he was taken to the end of time. He travels far and wide in heaven. His stamina increased. The eyes of John opened. You can't do networking of what will happen in the last day in ordinary manner. You must network with heaven.

Your prayer must be above asking bread and wine. You must network with heaven and grow in the spirit. When you pray and ascend in spirit you will be educated in the spirit. This is how it is done. Take this step to avoid error. Everybody doing things great today traveled far and wide. To be astounding you must network. If you know scripture, it is a gateway into the spirit realm. You must pray until something shift. You must pray until something happens. You must pray until miracles happen. This is how you conquer the battle of the age.

Our battle is not wisdom and knowledge or boldness. You must connect to the supernatural. David fought several battles and won all. He doesn't have the best army. Do you think it is ordinary? His fact is to enquire from God. He meets spirits in the spirit. This is spiritual networking. This is spiritual strategy used to fight and conquer in the spirit. You must strategize. Our advantage is in the spirit. If you pray to a level you break out of influence of time. If you are in the level where you pray out of time, all you will have is powerful downloaded version of reality.

You may not manifest until you meet your partner in the spirit. You pray and you will see the patriarchs. If you pray enough great doors will open, when you see people making things happen there is no coincidence about it. Our advantage is in the spirit. You will be a strategist in the battle field. When enemy are sleeping you will know. When they are weak, you will know. At their strength, you will know. When they move you will know, because you are saturated in the spirit. Those who did that which you are doing, you will have upper hand. They will hand over instruction manual to you. They will give strategies in the spirit to explore. They will give you freedom capsule energetic to make you fly high to conquer. Pray and pray, the spirit is saturated with powers of supernatural. Dig deep in prayer and excel. The battle at hand is a battle of mystery. It is a battle of supremacy. It is a battle of technology to soar high than eye can see.

There is assignment we cannot carry out with our training. There are assignments we can't carry out with our wisdom or understanding. We need heavenly touch. There must be spiritual networking. There are places you enter in the spirit you will come down with authority that will marvel you. You must pray and travel beyond the limitation of flesh. Prayer produces spiritual networking.

THE LION OF THE TRIBE OF JUDAH

PRAYER POINTS

1. Lord Jesus, thank you for your love for me and my family in the name of Jesus.
2. O Lord, forgive me, make good thing permanent in my life, I will not go back into sin.
3. Lord Jesus, I come before you, forgive me, in the name of Jesus.
4. I cover myself with blood of Jesus.
5. I drink blood of Jesus for healing and joy, in the name of Jesus.
6. Holy Spirit, network my prayer with heaven in the name of Jesus.
7. Holy Spirit, drag your net to the world and win souls into the kingdom in the name of Jesus.
8. O Lord, open my ears to understand the language of heaven in the name of Jesus.
9. Ability to pray and focus, come upon me, in the name of Jesus.

10. Spirit of lust; come out of me, in the name of Jesus.

11. Bread and wine shall not take over my glory in the name of Jesus.

12. Lion of Judah, trigger my prayer life, in the name of Jesus.

13. My heaven open, give me new ideas and discovery in the name of Jesus.

14. Every error that send one to hell, expire in my life, in the name of Jesus.

15. My gateway to success; open by fire in the name of Jesus.

16. Today, I climb my mountain of glory, in the name of Jesus.

17. Today, I climb mountain of success and breakthrough, in the name of Jesus.

18. O Lord, let me be a strategist to win in the battle field in the name of Jesus.

19. Every battle at the edge of breakthrough, scatter, in the name of Jesus.

20. Spirit of confusion in my life, quit my life, in the name of Jesus.
21. My soul shall not perish, in the name of Jesus.
22. Voice of heaven, speak to my life, in the name of Jesus.
23. Spirit of depression in me, expire, in the name of Jesus.
24. Plans of the enemy to keep me in bondage shall fail, in the name of Jesus.
25. My appetite for lust; expire, in the name of Jesus.
26. Dark power assign to edge me out in prayer, receive slap of Holy Ghost, in the name of Jesus.
27. O Lord, give me mantle to exploit the earth and make heaven in the name of Jesus.
28. Anointing of Elijah to live above sin flow in my life, in the name of Jesus.
29. I recover seven fold my wasted years in the name of Jesus.

30. My sacrifice to serve the Lord shall not be in vain, in the name of Jesus.
31. Satanic network design to destroy me; break in the name of Jesus.
32. Every gate of darkness assign against me; catch time and burn to ashes in the name of Jesus.
33. Every satanic crowd that gather against my prayer, scatter in the name of Jesus.
34. Witchcraft calendar and timetable for my life; catch fire and roast to ashes.
35. Witchcraft embargo of my father's house against my prayer, break in the name of Jesus.
36. My prayer life; re-ignite in the name of Jesus.
37. Come-and-go problem in my life, expire, in the name of Jesus.
38. I claim divine breakthrough and deliverance, in the name of Jesus.
39. Any power assign to turn my life upside down expire in the name of Jesus
40. Thou power of affliction troubling me, expire, in the name of Jesus.

41. Those who battle me shall bow before me, in the name of Jesus.

42. Foundational poverty troubling my life, expire, in the name of Jesus.

43. O heaven over my prosperity open by fire, in the name of Jesus.

44. Every Goliath, in my destiny, your time is up, die, in the name of Jesus.

45. Blood of Jesus, silence every power that vows to silence me, in the name of Jesus.

46. O Lord, let men and women begin to favor me, in the name of Jesus.

47. My enemies bow down to me and surrender in the name of Jesus.

48. Evil storm that rise against me expire, in the name of Jesus.

49. Every curse following me about, expire, in the name of Jesus.

50. Enough is enough; I possess my possession, in the name of Jesus.

51. Plans of the enemy against me scatter, in the name of Jesus.
52. Holy Spirit, fill up satanic grave dug for me in the spirit in the name of Jesus.
53. Satanic yoke of delay break in the name of Jesus.
54. Anointing of disgrace in my life, dry up in the name of Jesus.
55. Praise the Lord my problems are over, in the name of Jesus.

CHAPTER 4

HOW TO WALK IN THE SUPERNATURAL

Supernatural means superior to natural. When Enoch went to heaven it was supernatural. When Elijah went to heaven it was supernatural. When Jesus went to heaven it was supernatural. That is not the course to death. When in desolated land nothing good happens but when God pass through you, supernatural happens. You become a joy to many generations. Diverse healing, diverse impartation takes place in lives. Pray to sustain and administer in the supernatural. When you sustain you receive, when you administer, what you sustain, you administer to others. So you open your heart to sustain in order to administer to people around you and generation. This is how the Lion in you wakes up and pushes you beyond knowledge. As you administer, you grow strong and strong.

When man was created he was created in the envelope of supernatural. Before God created the earth he dwells in the invisible realm. God is the creator. The first creation is the spirits but he wants to advance the creation of invisible realm. For this cause he called forth immateriality into materiality (for deep understanding of this buy my book titled **Command the day**). What we call supernatural is the ability to impose one realm on another. When what happen in the invisible realm is converted to physical it becomes supernatural. Supernatural means superior to the natural. So when Enoch went to heaven it is supernatural, because in heaven physical body doesn't exist. When Jesus ascended the body entered heaven it is supernatural.

When a man walks in the supernatural realm he has the ability to download the things invisible into visible. Supernatural is not a story or theory it is manifestation of invisible; until its manifestation is seen everything you do is inconclusive. A time will come when believers will live supernatural. It is when a man walks with God and do not sick. On earth men fall sick but you are not sick. This is supernatural. When a man walks on earth and not limited by the powers of time, it is supernatural. That is why when God created Adam he put him in Eden. Eden was a portal, a bridge that connects earth to heaven. Adam has opportunity to enter the invisible realm, but failed. He could have been the first to enter the invisible realm if he got well with God. He was carried away with the splendor in the Garden. God visits him in the evening every day. He was carried away until one day he ate the forbidden fruit. He was not smart enough he should be the first to ascend to heaven. He didn't take advantage of what was available to him until he ate the forbidden fruit and was kicked out of the garden.

This is the reason you don't factor sin to life in the house of God the Eden of today. That miracle happens in your church doesn't mean everybody have access to miracle. You must obey the heavenly rules of the game through prayer and fasting. Avoid lust it erodes destiny, sin makes you empty and naked before God. You won't hear voice of God anymore as it was with Adam. So let the spirit of Lion keeps you awake. Know what is wrong and do the right thing. Pray and not be lukewarm. Gather momentum to visit the heavenly and tap power.

The irony of life is, many don't take advantage of what they have. Adam was one of such. He had the advantage to go in and out with God to heaven but never use it, only God come in the evening. He lost opportunity open to him. He never discovered the spirit of Lion in him. You have heavenly talent to explore the earth but most time loses it. In the church you don't belong to any group. You don't pray, you hardly fast to receive revelation. You attend service only on Sundays. Your mind is lost even during service. What a gap between you and God? And you expect the Lion in you to roar. Is it possible? I am not sure.

When God created Adam he said go and multiply and fill the earth. We always interpret it to mean, "Sleep with Eve and bear children" "Take control of what I created, have money, build houses and enjoy yourself" What God actually wanted of him is to link with the supernatural realm and do the replica in heaven on earth. It means super impose heaven into earth until earth is replica of heaven. What God wants Adam to do is to download heaven to earth. Eden was not earth, it is not heaven. Eden is a point that connects spirit realm to the natural realm. God kept Adam there with a choice. If you want to journey to heaven, that is your choice. Adam had the right and the power to enter into the invisible realm. He would have been the first man to enter the spirit realm bodily but that wasn't Adam's priority.

What God wanted Adam to do is to download heaven on earth. Eden was not created; Eden was down loaded from heaven. The book of **Ezekiel 28:13** confirms it *"Thou hast been in Eden the garden of God; every precious stone was thy covering, the sardius, topaz, and the diamond, the beryl, the onyx, and the jasper, the sapphire, the emerald, and the carbuncle, and gold: the workmanship of thy tabrets and of thy pipes was prepared in thee in the day that thou wast created."* This is where Lucifer stays. What God want Adam to do is to spread-forth Eden in heaven from on earth; instead Adam was kicked out. This is how some people behave when they can't manage what is given to them. It is taken from them and another takes over. Adam lost! It was at the point he lost, Jesus starts. This is why Satan challenged him thrice in temptation.

When Jesus defeated Satan he went out in glory doing good. If Adam has allowed spirit of God to dwell in him, he would have explored the earth. But he failed. The spirit of a Lion was not found in him. When Jesus came he explored Eden and around it. Miracles flow in him. Mercy and favor were found in him. He downloads the invisible realm to the visible realm. The power Adam lost, he applied in the new garden. Jesus started where Adam stop. We read he was doing well what he did was ability to bring what is in the heaven to natural realm. When Jesus came to a woman who suffered for 12 years, he said to the woman "thou art loose". To the leper he healed. To the blind he gave sight. To the paralytic he made whole. What the first Adam lost, the second Adam gained. He gained fame and glory. The spirit of Lion in him roared and miracle happened. Jesus came from Zion and was supernatural. He is a life giving spirit. His job is to reign in invisible dimension until the visible realm is explored. He came to correct the error of first Adam.

We are not here to survive but dominate. If you are living to survive but not dominate you lose. If you are living to survive you don't know the purpose of existence, you fail. We are not here to survive we are the representative of the invisible God. When you find a family, God expect the family to be a nucleus in heaven. When you find a society, God expect that society will become a nucleus in heaven. Unfortunately we are at loss. Not every family or society aligns with heaven. They chase the shadow.

We must awake to find the blue print of existence. Speak to your hand, speak to your family. Speak to your linage. Speak to your nation. How do you do this?, from the altar in your house. You can superimpose heaven in your family. You can superimpose heaven to your destiny. When you do, quarrel, sickness, death, poverty will vanish. You supper impose heaven on them. It is time to arise and do what the heavens need and approve so that we live heaven on earth.

It is time to talk righteousness to live and exterminates iniquity. It's time to apply the light in Jesus and shut down the gates open to sickness and disease because we are the hope the world is looking for. The hope of the world is not out there. The hope is your contribution in prayer to save the land from the hands of aliens that vow darkness will rule and dominate us. Where is the lion in you to bring the supernatural into the natural realm? The world is hopeless, it is dying.

There are ways of controlling and manifesting the supernatural. Exploration of the world is borderless; age is not a barrier, color is not a barrier, your location is not a barrier. Jesus at 12 years questioned the doctors at law in the synagogue. The question they couldn't answer, he gives answer. When God uses you other impediments vanish. Your access to the kingdom saves the day.

Empower yourself in the supernatural with mystery of height. Your height in the spirit determines your power over the enemy. It is said, I am above not below. To be above is to occupy great height, or supernatural height to explore the earth. The spirit of lion takes you to greater height. Height in the spirit is authority. When you occupy great height, you bring the supernatural to the natural. Occupying height in the spirit is a factor to know God. He is called the Most High, because he controls higher realm. For him to control the entire realm he must be the Most High. And everyone who wants to have authority must be a high man. You must be high to take authority and walk into the realm of glory.

For you to wield power you must go high. **Isaiah 14:12-14** says: *"How you are fallen from heaven, O Lucifer, son of the morning! How you are cut* *down to the ground, you who weakened the nations! For you have said in your heart: I will ascend into heaven; I will exalt my throne above the stars of God; I will also sit on the mount of the congregation on the farthest sides of the north; I will ascend above the heights of the clouds, I will be like the Most High."*

In the angelic realm it is known that power is a factor of height. He knows that power is a factor of height. He knows authority is not a dress code. It is a height base reality. Authority is not how you squeeze your face. It doesn't move men and women anymore. Anybody can squeeze face. You can cast out demons with smiles and not squeeze face. It is the authority you carry that matters. Let the spirit of lion in you awake with authority and cast out devil.

Authority doesn't include sweat. Sweat is a function of heat evaporating in the body. Power is height oriented. When Satan said, "I will ascend--

above the stars" The star is the angelic power that gives you authority to control the angel. It is the height you occupy and operate from. *"You said in your heart, "I will ascend into heaven! I will exalt my throne above the stars of God! I will sit on the mountain of assembly, in the far north!"* **Isaiah 14:13.** A man who wants to walk in the supernatural must pay the price to begin to understand the reality of heavenly places. You may sit in heavenly places but not perceive the reality.

Theologically speaking you sit with Christ but experientially speaking you are not because you don't exercise the authority. Your experience and power is the expression of your perception. If you don't perceive the reality that is there though you are there you won't use it. It is a man with frequency of right antenna will down load it. We are all seated with Christ in heavenly places but few of us understand it. You must engage the spirit to perceive before you can function. All of us can call the name of Jesus and quote bible verses. When we come to demon not everyone overcome. The person in the height among us will tackle the problem right. Others will just be shouting and sweat but no answer. The reason is they are not at the height to control and overpower the demon. The man who works in the supernatural is the man who is in the height. You may sit in heavenly places but not perceive the height you occupy.

Pastors may quote the bible but nothing happens. They refuse to ask the question; "What shall I do"? This is the question our generation refuses to ask. It is where you are in height that gives what you can do. If you are a child in the spirit, you can do little. Upgrade yourself spiritually and command authority. Elijah clashed with King Ahab and fled from Jezebel. In the spirit he decree there shall be no rain or dew. It came to pass. If you don't gain height you will be ridiculed. For forty days he journey to Horeb. When he stood on Horeb something happened. The bible says the Lord passed by him, he heard the sound of earthquake; the sound of fire; the Lord was not there. It is when you gain height you will know reality.

Elijah was in the height with supernatural spirit. You may be seated with Christ but when there is fear you are on the floor. Experientially speaking you are not, because you don't exercise the authority. When a man succeeds in climbing the place of glory and place of height he occupies a place of stillness. It is when you gain height you can tell the difference between reality. There is a place you get to you know there is salvation of God. The moment there is turbulence in your spirit you have not ascended. You may be sited with Christ so long there is fear and uncertainty you are on the floor. When we say gain height we are telling you a place you get to where you are powerful to see the salvation of God. It was James that says the 40 days of Elijah was not just physical journey but a journey of prayer. That means the mystery of height is mystery of prayer.

That prayer is not a casual prayer. It is a prayer done with Holy Spirit. The reason is because every man has dimensions it operates. You may have bodily dimension where anxiety dwells, you may have bodily dimension where fear dwells, you may have bodily dimension where wickedness dwells. There are divine dimensions. You have both spirit and flesh dimensions. They said Christ in you the hope of glory. Prayer travels from bodily dimension to divine dimension. When praying you leave a realm beyond capacity. When they tell you your landlord will kick you out tomorrow you are at peace. If you are still in bodily dimension; anxiety will kill you unless you have ascended.

When Jesus wants to ascend he goes to pray. It is written, he took Peter, James and John to mountain to pray. When he went solitary to pray, Elijah and Moses joined him. The cloud of glory came down and covered him. When he came down the disciples were battling with a boy that was possessed. Meanwhile, before that time he has given them power, they went out, they cast out demon and were celebrating. This little boy gave them spiritual headache until Jesus who gained height came down. He ordered the boy should be brought to him. He rebuked the demon and it left him. The disciples were amazed and ask why they couldn't rebuke the demon. He said it needs fasting and prayer. It is not ordinary fasting and prayer, but that which is of man that gained height. Jesus has higher authority. The disciples were talking from location of uncertainty and fear, but Jesus knew nothing like that, he spoke from location of authority.

Just like Moses, when he came back from the mountain, his eyes changed to eyes of fire. When he was challenged, he said let the earth open and swallow the accusers. He is in a different realm.

Who told him the earth has a mouth that swallows. Moses acted like a man of God, "Let earth open and swallow my distractors" was his vadict. He commands the gangsters to be on one side and said what had not happened before will happen today. The earth open and swallow them. Do you have confidence in the Lord? Do you thirst and hunger for prayer? This is the act that can wake the spirit of Lion in you. Exercise the spirit and disgrace the enemy that vow to shame you.

When you enter the glory you will see the code of nature. When you enter the glory you can see the blue print of nature. Moses can see far, in the realm everything is possible. If you are like Moses you won't fear, because the Lord will show you great and mighty things. ***"Call unto me, and I will answer thee, and shew thee great and mighty things, which thou knowest not."*** **Jeremiah 33:3.** Can you surrender to God to show you great and mighty thing. Open your heart to the spirit of the Lion of the tribe of Judah.

You will see more than you bargain for, if you pray. Our problem is we don't travel in the spirit in prayer. If you want to handle the supernatural you must travel. There are things you will see you don't know. There are things beyond realm of understanding except you engage in supernatural travels. Speak in tongues. It is not foolishness, power is embedded in it. As you do it, migration begins to take place, light shines in darkness and every secret is revealed. I prophesy, you will not know limitation. Your result will shock everyone around you.

Sometimes you have to pray for weeks or months. The more you pray, the more you travel in the spirit. The more you travel in spirit, the more you gain height and occupy territory of authority. You are far ahead of mountain of life and occupy mountain of Zion. You will have assurance no man can take away from you. Ascend in prayer before you leave home. Nothing will move you or take you unaware. This is how Jesus lives; he goes to solitary places to pray. When he is done nothing comes to him unaware. If you like come as cripple, come blind, be a leper, be tormented by demons, he doesn't care. He is fully loaded. He commands and decree and get result.

When you gain height in the spirit, you will notice the hand of God. Jesus works from heaven. He is in spirit because he went to solitary places to pray. He ascends before he comes out. Others come out from their house but Jesus comes out from his glory with authority. Nothing moves him. Nothing shakes him unaware. When the disciples were persecuted they went into solitary place in company and prayed. As they raised their voices to God, they enquired God to stretch hand upon them with power to heal and perform miraculous signs and wonders through the name of Jesus. After they prayed the place they prayed shakes. They were filled with Holy Spirit and spoke the word of God boldly (**Acts 4:23-31**).

Demon don't read book; he talks from the height as well. He has authority as well. His authority is backed by Lucifer. He was created before you were born. So, before you can defeat him in battle you must speak from the height with Jesus. In his name, creatures in heaven, earth and beneath the earth bow. He is of the tribe of the Lion of Judah. How many books did sorcerer read? How many books did herbalist read? They know the technology to ascend even it is demonic. They wield authority. They go far into the forest or into the coven chanting incantations until they are soaked in power.

How many books did rituals in your village read when they are intoxicated they enter their element, they are in the realm. It is at this level they enter the town. And you that cram few scriptures in the bible will jump up and say you want to bind. Bind who? You are on the ground, not even standing but asleep. The man is charged. The man is high. The man is volatile in evil kingdom. You must pray and bring him down in prayer. Not ice-cream prayer but volatile, warfare and deadly prayers. It is at this point, the spirit of lion of Judah roar in you.

You will notice the hand of God when you pray. The hand of God is supernatural but it is for those who understand it. If you pray from the earth you will be defeated. The spirit is mountain being. If you don't ascend higher you can't defeat them. You will get to a height your country will be too small to handle. Pray to be global. There is a height you get to, to download something to the earth. The higher you are in spirit, the better for you. If you are on ground motor can stop you, train can stop you. Herds of cow can stop you. Soldier can stop you. Police can stop you. Mountain can stop you. But when you go higher and far up in the spirit, you will experience traffic flow with frequency of answer to good antenna. You want to journey in the supernatural? You must journey in the spirit. You must pray a robust praying energy to attain it.

You must occupy good height in prayer for a long time. This is what you do to occupy the spirit realm and manipulate the enemy in the spirit realm and lay legislation. You will know what to say and when to say it. If you carry anointing of healing and you don't pray, sickness will kill you. If you carry anointing of breakthrough and you don't journey in prayer, you will die in debt and be poor. It is when you understand life and gain height in prayer, you will conquer. When you journey high and pass it to your children it becomes inheritance.

It doesn't stop there; you must walk in the light. There is a height you must function from before faith commits you to a place of obedient. It is the strength of your obedience that determines your prayer. You don't know when prayer is so difficult. If you want to pray demon will do everything to distract you. They know if you start praying even if you are illiterate you have authority than them. Whatever language you speak, demon will obey. It is not responding to your language, it is responding to your thought. If you have authority they interpret your thought. Your thought is there command. Mere looking at your face they know what you mean and where you are in the spirit realm. Jesus appeared in the Gadarenes, the demon shouted and pleaded with Jesus even before Jesus spoke! The demons in him said "Please send us into this swine", they protested. It is the power and authority of Jesus they recognized. Authority is a game. When you pray or command and spend hours on an issue it shows you don't have enough authority. A man loaded with authority may get to where you are sweating in prayer to cast out demon. He gives command and the sick becomes well. And suddenly the demons obey. Such person spent hours, days and weeks building height in the secret. And when loaded with power he step out, he has authority. What take hours, takes him a moment. Invest in prayer. What takes you weeks to solve can take you a day. What takes you days, can take you a second. Prayer is powerful. It depends on where you are praying from.

If you find man who walks in the supernatural he is flooded with light. What is light? Light is the revelation knowledge of the word of God. The bible said in the beginning was the word. *"In the beginning was the Word, and the Word was with God, and the Word was God. The same was in the beginning with God. All things were made by him; and without him was not anything made that was made. In him was life; and the life was the light of men. And the light shineth in*

darkness; and the darkness comprehended it not." **John 1:1-5.**

The word of God becomes your light. If you walk in the light the power of God responds. If you walk in the light, it provokes power. You need light to move in power. Jesus was the Word but until he became light he has no authority.

Until you see the light or walk in light you can't see the supernatural. Supernatural responds to light. Your mind, your emotion, your will are controlled by word of God. If your mind, will and emotion are not controlled by word of God, you can't walk in the supernatural. If your word is at variance with light, your word becomes helpless. While prayer is a product of transition, light is a product of transformation. When you talk or preach it is light that transform you or made you known. The light exposes you. If word of God doesn't have authority over you, it can't have authority through you. You live by word to operate by word. What this mean is your word must mean something to you. Be transparent and abide by your word in the spirit. It is at this level you can operate with word in the spirit. There is nothing like African time as a Christian. When you say, I will be around at 4 0' clock pm. Let it be. If you say call me at 3 0' clock pm and you are called but you don't pick, you don't live by your word. If you don't keep your word with men, you won't do it to God. If you are not worthy of word, you can't go far in the spirit. You can't use your word to cast out demon.

You are a servant of the word. Follow your word to letter. Word means life and death. A man that drinks alcohol won't flow in the spirit to conquer demons. There is life and death in the tongue. Watch your tongue. If you understand the power of word you won't speak negative words jokingly or seriously no matter the condition or situation. Such are garbage we pick in the society, it is bad. You can't invoke heaven for answer. What you hear becomes energy in your spirit. What is in you is different from what is in your lip. When you quote the scripture demon is interested in what you are. Any man who is serious in supernatural doesn't play with his word. He doesn't say careless word.

PRAYER POINTS

1. O Lord, I thank you for your wonderful love for me, in the name of Jesus.
2. I thank you Lord for delivering my soul from untimely death, in the name of Jesus.
3. Angels of God, support me, in the name of Jesus.
4. Blood of Jesus, wash me clean, in the name of Jesus.
5. O Lord, forgive my sins and prosper me in all sides in the name of Jesus.

6. Holy Spirit, fill me to serve the Lord, in the name of Jesus.
7. I conquer and rule in the supernatural, in the name of Jesus.
8. Spirit of Enoch to walk in the Lord be my portion in the name of Jesus.
9. The mistake of Eden to disobey God shall not happen in my life in the name of Jesus.
10. O Lord, visit me as in the beginning, in the name of Jesus.
11. Lust shall not erode my destiny, in the name of Jesus.
12. O Lord, let your fire consume dark powers after my life, in the name of Jesus.
13. Anointing to move forward, flow in my life, in the name of Jesus.
14. Every padlock assign against my prayer life, break to pieces in the name of Jesus.
15. Every Satanic gang up against my destiny, scatter in the name of Jesus.

THE LION OF THE TRIBE OF JUDAH

16. Strangers waging war against my prayer life, expire, in the name of Jesus.
17. O Lord, let me enjoy every advantage that come my way, in the name of Jesus.
18. O Lord, I am ready to serve you, be with me, in the name of Jesus.
19. My heaven open and favor me in the name of Jesus.
20. I super-impose heaven into my destiny, in the name of Jesus.
21. I super-impose heaven into my marriage for signs and wonders in the name of Jesus.
22. Spirit of quarrel and fight, leave me alone, I surrender to Christ in the name of Jesus.
23. Arrow of sickness and disease fired against me backfire in the name of Jesus.
24. Heavenly righteousness, locate me by fire in the name of Jesus.
25. Lion of Judah, turn supernatural blessing to natural blessing now, in the name of Jesus.

26. Power of darkness in my life, clear away in the name of Jesus.

27. O Lord, take me to great height of champion in the name of Jesus.

28. O Lord, send down fire against enemies of my soul, in the name of Jesus.

29. O Lord, frustrate and scatter wicked plans of the enemy against me, in the name of Jesus.

30. Every contrary power pursuing me about, stop by fire in the name of Jesus.

31. Father Lord, let Holy Spirit, fill me afresh in the name of Jesus.

32. O Lord, catapult my spiritual life to the mountain top in the name of Jesus.

33. Desolate land in my destiny be converted to breakthrough, in the name of Jesus.

34. O Lord, grant me victory over temptation in the name of Jesus.

35. I shall not fish in unprofitable waters in the name of Jesus.

THE LION OF THE TRIBE OF JUDAH

36. I wash and clean marks of sin in my life by the power in the blood of Jesus.
37. Holy Ghost fire; incubate my spirit life, in the name of Jesus.
38. I will cause joy and happiness to expand in my generation, in the name of Jesus.
39. I withdraw my steps from evil places in the name of Jesus.
40. I receive fresh fire to move forward in life, in the name of Jesus.
41. Demonic sleep troubling my life, end by fire in the name of Jesus.
42. Whatever will take God from me, expire, in the name of Jesus.
43. Whoever will take God from me, expire, in the name of Jesus.
44. I receive power to walk in the spirit, in the name of Jesus.
45. I wear garment of righteousness in the name of Jesus.
46. O Lord, hold me to you in the name of Jesus.

47. O Lord, renew a right spirit within me, in the name of Jesus.

48. Every wound in my life, receive divine healing, in the name of Jesus.

49. Dark lion after me, be devoured by the Lion of Judah.

50. I will prosper and never fail in the name of Jesus.

51. O Lord; move me from minimum to maximum level of greatness in the name of Jesus.

52. Blockage and barriers against me are over now and forever more, in the name of Jesus. Amen.

CHAPTER 5

THE ANOINTING OF THE HOLY SPIRIT

The anointing of the Holy Spirit speaks volume in the life of believers. You need Holy Spirit in the journey of life. There is competition in the world. There is bustle and hustle all over. There are two phases on earth; the kingdom of Satan which represents darkness, and the kingdom of God which represents light. The same way God raise people to build church, the same way Satan raise men to build house of darkness like night clubs. Both are worship centers. The church is a worship center for God of heaven; the other is a worship center for Satan. The church is a selfless act of humanity; Satan's centers are act of selfishness and wickedness. There is battle in the spirit realm to lure your steps to the world and end up in hell fire. This is where you need Holy Spirit to take control so that you end up as Lion of the tribe of Judah.

Pray that God works in your life by the spirit of the anointing of the Holy Ghost. AT times your hard work, diligence, smartness seems things are not working as plan. Hope is not filled to the ability put in. Today, God will function with you by the anointing of the spirit. It is on record you must work hard to succeed. To work is good but there is a power that serves as catalyst in the spirit to promote hard work. It is not only by hard work a man succeeds. Really, hard work is necessary, so are diligence and other factors. As Christian, there is an edge you have over others, and that is Holy Spirit. He gives you advantage in all situations.

Idol worshippers also work hard. The atheists that don't believe in existence of God also work hard. These categories work smartly and diligently. They put effort in what they do. There is edge you have as a believer. There is power you know they don't know, and it is good you hold tight to it. It is Holy Spirit. If all you have is of the world you will fail. There are many people who work harder. If you think you are a warehouse of intelligence, there are people with ships of intelligence. In all, you are not discouraged to work hard or smartly. Wake your heart to consciousness that upgrade and give spiritual support in all you do. It is the power that promotes and ensures you are a Lion in the in the supernatural realm. You go far in life when you take advantage of what you possess.

Brethren, understand this, when you look around. There are professors who put 30 years in service but couldn't point at capital venture of their own. There are men of God laboring in the vineyard of God without improvement. There are business men and women who toil day and night but couldn't make end meet. In addition to hard work, in addition to diligence, in addition to smart work there is an edge that a believer has, that edge is the anointing of the Holy Spirit.

This is a power we look down because we don't see it or believe it. This spirit guides you, guides your speech, guides your action and then makes you a champion. Anointing of Holy Spirit makes you understand the advantage you have in life. To explore the spirit of Lion of Judah add Holy Spirit to everything you do. You need Holy Spirit to succeed. Jesus trained his disciples for three years and they wanted to go out and do what their master did. They had training and experience, yet before they go out Jesus said tarry until the Holy Spirit come upon you. Jesus promise Holy Spirit will visit them and turn them around for exploit.

Without Holy Spirit you may not go far. Tarry in prayer, tarry in songs of heaven, far from sin, for Holy Spirit. Holy Spirit is advantage you have in life. If you don't take advantage of what God gives you and go outside you will fail. The absence of Holy Spirit in your life will not make things work. Qualification is not a yardstick, experience is not confirmation you won't fail, wealth or good capital at hand doesn't me you will make it, if you don't have Holy Spirit that guides you.

Let Holy Spirit dwell in you in full; else you go nowhere. There is advantage you have, if you don't take the advantage you will be stagnant or disappear in the race of life. Even if you qualify things won't work because you don't take advantage of the Holy Spirit. Toil without Holly Spirit is a disadvantage or else battles of life will swallow you. ***"Who gave himself for our sins, that he might deliver us from this present evil world, according to the will of God and our Father"*** **Galatians 1:4** You can work hard still people will be angry with you for no reason. And that person will make it his responsibility to make sure you go nowhere. Unless spirit of Lion of Judah rules you things may be difficult. If not, enemy will deal with you and deal with your children. You will be wandering to ask "What have I done". You don't need to wrong anybody. It is their evil pattern of wickedness. You need advantage, that advantage is called the anointing of Holy Spirit. Wealth comes from the Holy Spirit, poverty comes from Satan. With anointing of Holy Spirit doors of opportunity will open, and you begin to laugh and be happy.

Open your heart to Holy Spirit to operate. Discern his word and command. He may command you to start a particular business, hearken to his voice. Where you think nothing works, he is there for you to make things work. It is you that need to wake the spirit of Lion in you to encourage and boost your morale. When anointing come upon Jesus in the Jordan River, three and half years became important than 30 years before he started his ministry. You may think you have been blessed wait for anointing of the Holy Spirit to proof you wrong. Thank God for your diligence. Thank God for your hard work. Thank God, I say, thank God.

Yet you need advantage of Holy Spirit to stir the ship of your life to a cool and profitable destination.

How do you receive anointing? It is simple, you ask for it. The Bible says, ask you will receive, seek you will find, knock the door will open to you. ***"Ask and it will be given to you; seek and you will find; knock and the door will be opened to you. For everyone who asks receives; the one who seeks finds; and to the one who knocks, the door will be opened."* Matthew 7:7-8.** The reason people lose is, they go wrong direction. Some people put energy in what they do; they don't succeed because they never ask God to help them. They complain, than ask God for direction and help. They complain, the country is hard, the town is hard, people hate them, and people ridicule them or mock them. There is no how you ask God with sincerity and you are denied. Jesus asks who among you will ask his father for bread and will give him stone or fish and give him fish. If you ask the father he will give you Holly Spirit, the spirit that discerns the spirit to hear heaven, the spirit that energizes spirit of Lion in you.

The problem is, most of us don't ask for the anointing and God stays there waiting for us. Wake the spirit of Lion in you to walk you into paradise of achievement. The Lord is sober for your sake. He asks how I wish you ask me. The prodigal son left home and squandered his inheritance in a far land but retraced his step back home and seeks forgiveness. The spirit of Lion in him wake his sense to go back home. He repented and obeyed the voice of Holy Spirit. He cried before his father and asked for forgiveness and acceptance into his father's house. The father did, and organized party for him. They ate and were filled. What the prodigal son did was, he asks and was given a listening ear. His senior brother that toiled with his father when he left was jealous. He went to his father and complained and said, "My brother lavished his inheritance abroad and came back, and you organized elaborate party but never did such for me". The father said he didn't forget him. The summary of it all is, the prodigal son asks for forgiveness and acceptance. This is the pillar, ask! The prodigal son was not prodigal in asking, he was prodigal in spending. Most men, who make impact in life, are good at asking. Keep asking God, don't say "It is too much, how will he do it?" This is the reason; he is called El-Shadai, the all sufficient God. Keep asking, and keep doing the right thing in his sight. Ask and obtain from God. When you are going for businesses ask. When you are going to office ask. When you are going into ministry ask. When you are going into marriage ask. One of the secret of overcoming is they know how to ask.

To be a Lion in the spirit, you must live far from sin. Sin is a capsule of untimely death. Sin declares you absent in God's presence. Jesus welcomes you as his, if you confess your sin. *"If you declare with your mouth, "Jesus is Lord," and believe in your heart that God raised him from the dead, you will be saved."* **Romans 10:9.** It is one thing to receive; it is another thing to walk in it. If you are in the spirit, walk in the spirit. If you have money and do not spend it, you do not walk in it. If you have inheritance and do not make use of it, you didn't walk in it. You don't need a pastor to lay hand on you before you take a move. Don't drag your breakthrough in the mud. You don't need prophet to decree over you. If the Lion in you wake to action you will be surprise of the anointing in your life.

You must be conscious of Holy Spirit. If you don't have the consciousness the anointing won't activate. It is not every time you go to preach you prepare. There are times you have close schedule. But as you climb pulpit, the Lord's spirit arrests the situation. Have the conscience of I am the head and not the tail. It is spirit that awakens consciousness that makes the Lion in you vibrate. In the Bible Paul know the meaning of spiritual consciousness. He was invited for a deliverance he could not go, he sent his handkerchief to them and immediately the handkerchief was applied on the sick he was made whole. *"So that from his body were brought unto the sick handkerchiefs or aprons, and the diseases departed from them, and the evil spirits went out of them."* **Acts 19:12.**

Jesus knows the meaning of consciousness. In the temple, he said the spirit of the Lord is upon me. *"The Spirit of the Lord is upon me, because he hath anointed me to preach the gospel to the poor; he hath sent me to heal the brokenhearted, to preach deliverance to the captives, and recovering of sight to the blind, to set at liberty them that are bruised."* **Luke 4:18**. Jesus know there is anointing upon him. It is with this consciousness he healed the sick. He opens the eyes of the blind. He healed the paralytic. He drove out demons because there is anointing of Holy Spirit upon him. When you speak and lay hands upon your children, you are conscious of the Holy Spirit in you.

To be a champion belief you are not the one in charge, it is the Holy Spirit. Your body is controlled by the Holy Spirit. Whatever happens never says you did it. Have the testament you brought God to the scene and to the ring. This is how the lion in you operates. You are not the one fighting anymore. God fights on your account. The error of people is they leave God behind and fight for themselves. Whenever anything confronts you bring God on the scene. You heard of high blood pressure, migraine, hypertension, cancer; tell anybody that care to hear you that your body is the temple of God. What will harm will first harm Jesus. And Jesus came to this world to save you of infirmity, curse and every negative. You can't be brought down. Holy Ghost dwells in your body. If Holy Ghost dwells in your body, cancer cannot kill you. Diabetes cannot kill you. You are not the owner of your body there is a spirit that is in you, the spirit is Holy Spirit. The Spirit is the spirit of the Lion of Judah. If you doubt pray to God to open your eyes in the order of Gehazi when enemies encompass them. God open his eyes to see the battalion of heavenly soldiers against the enemy. Gehazi was in doubt, this is the reason Elijah said God should open his eyes. Elijah did not fear because he knows the anointing he carries. David knows the anointing he carries this is the reason he said, "Though I walk in the valley of the shadow of death I fear no evil". He walks with smile not fear. He believes he won't perish, the Lord is with him. Behave and believe as David. He enters every mission with the Holy Spirit and fear not. If God is for you who can be against you? David said by my God I run through a troop. By my God I leap over a wall. Don't fear, you come with the Lion of the tribe of Judah. You come with a warrior the Lord of Host. You came with El-Elion.

Pray for Holy Spirit to dwell in you. When others are thinking circumstances will engulf them, you are thinking how you will give testimony. David never went down before bear, he killed it and share testimony. He did not fraternize before Goliath, he killed him and share testimony. You are weak because you think you are alone. There are people that see themselves in coffin when they are told they have cancer; while some will think how they will give testimony. You are two different people in the same situation. To some who are in debt, one will think how he sinks in debt, while another think how he will grow and give testimony. The problem with the weak is he thought he is alone and is dejected. This should not be if you possess the spirit of the Lion of Judah. The things that throw some men down, when you think it, you will be thinking of testimony because you believe in anointing of the Holy Spirit. The anointing you carry punctures darkness in you and clears it away. Suddenly authority comes upon you, and you begin to move.

The spirit in you must support existence of Holy Spirit in your life. Never speak faithless word. Build faith, speak faith and act faith. Don't doubt you will have what you say. This is the reason you don't speak evil to yourself. Satan records it and will use it against you. The spirit of Lion in you is weak and wounded. It can't fight back when Satan arise to deal with you. You can kill the spirit of God in you with mouth as did children of Israel when the 12 spies went to spy the Promised Land. Ten of them brought fearful reports that they are like grasshopper before the Philistines who are like giants. Only Joshua and Caleb disagreed and told the congregation to prepare to take over the land.

The ten spies were judged to die with the congregations that listened to them except youths among them. This is how you kill the spirit in you with fear. When you pursue big thing, think big! ***"When men are cast down, then thou shalt say, there is lifting up; and he shall save the humble person."* Job 22:29.** God will confirm what you say.

If you want to see change by the word you say you are at the mercy of your word and the change you are looking for, you are at the mercy of your word. You are a king and priest; and where a king is there is power. When a king talks fear he will have fear but when a king talks victory whether the enemy likes it or not he will succeed. You encourage your children to excel. You encourage your spouse to excel, so is your community, town or nation. There is power in what you say and do. Build moral all the time. When you talk yourself down, you go down. Your spirit goes down, the

Lion shivers. Your strength goes down. But when you activate the anointing of the Holy Spirit, your life begin to change, even you have taken action.

The direction of the world is iniquity. It kills the spirit of Lion and reduces you in the spirit. When you click on things of the world, you see million clicks, but clicks what promotes word of God you can't find million. Anything that comes from demonic realm goes naturally viral. Do you know, big men of God in the pulpit with crowds of millions don't have followers of musicians in the internet? The world goes for worldly things that are short lived. Where are celebrities of the past? They are forgotten eaten by worms, but Jesus name and works is as new as yester years.

Musicians and celebrities sing worldly songs without Christ. They pull crowd and are popular for a while. They steal the spirits of many and sink in the pit of life. Only those who know heaven is real keep to themselves and never fall. They nurse and keep the spirit of Lion in them strong. They don't mess about but keep growing in the Lord. Those in the crowd lack spiritual intelligence. They are not alone, but are Pastors, teachers, prophets, evangelists, apostles who are in the dark world. They eat, mingle, and covenant with witchcraft. This is why you pray, fast and has discernment.

Let Holy Spirit dwell in you. What you say, come from the heart. If what you preach or says is ungodly, your heart is polluted. Your spirit is weak of Holy Spirit. What emit are pride, arrogance, wickedness and evil. Utterances is powerful, there is a spirit backing it. You need salvation to forge ahead and be a champion.

PRAYER POINTS

1. O Lord, thank you for your anointing upon my life in the name of Jesus.
2. Lord Jesus, thank you for your love and goodness in my life, in the name of Jesus.
3. O Lord, forgive me so that your anointing will flow in my life.
4. Blood of Jesus, flow in my life, from my head to my toes in the name of Jesus.
5. I drink blood of Jesus for strength and vitality, in the name of Jesus.
6. Holy Spirit, be my partner in all I do, in the name of Jesus.
7. Anointing of Holy Spirit come upon me in the name of Jesus.
8. Satanic kingdom around me I pull you down in the name of Jesus.
9. Anointing of God promote my hand work in the name of Jesus.

10. Siege of the enemy against me break, in the name of Jesus.
11. Anointing of God, break the chains that bind me, in the name of Jesus.
12. Anointing of God nullify anything done in the spirit to pollute me in the name of Jesus.
13. I reverse every satanic calendar against my anointing in the name of Jesus.
14. I bind every negative energy in the spirit working against me, in the name of Jesus.
15. I shall live above hardship in the name of Jesus.
16. Efforts of wasters to waste my life shall backfire at them in the name of Jesus.
17. Holy Spirit, empower me to have edge over my enemy and competitors in the name of Jesus.
18. Covenant of wealth; be fulfilled in my life, in the name of Jesus.
19. Every council of witchcraft working against my anointing, expire, in the name of Jesus.
20. I release myself from witchcraft cage, in the name of Jesus.

21. Anointing of God in my life promote integrity and favor me in the name of Jesus.
22. Evil seeds planted in the plantation of my life, wither, in the name of Jesus.
23. Every strongman assigned to rubbish my anointing be terminated in the name of Jesus.
24. Evil arrow against my destiny, backfire to the sender, in the name of Jesus.
25. Every obstacle in my life, give way to miracle, in the name of Jesus.
26. Anointing of God, break the power of limitation in my life, in the name of Jesus.
27. My destiny arise, move to next level of breakthrough in the name of Jesus.
28. O God arises; let my shame and sorrow expire, in the name of Jesus.
29. O God arises, fill my mouth with laughter of anointing in the name of Jesus.
30. Anointing of God upon my head, destroy power manipulating my life, in the name of Jesus.

31. Engine of prayer, occupy my heart in the name of Jesus.

32. I will sing my song and dance my dance to the glory of God upon my life.

33. Lord Jesus, do something new in my life in the name of Jesus.

34. My prayer life shall not dry in the name of Jesus.

35. Witchcraft eyes monitoring my life go blind, in the name of Jesus.

36. O Lord, let my testimony manifest in the name of Jesus.

37. No evil word from the sun, the moon or the star shall tarnish my anointing, in the name of Jesus.

38. I will fulfill my destiny whether the enemy likes it or not in the name of Jesus.

39. Warring angels around me awake the spirit of Lion in me, in the name of Jesus.

40. Anointing of God upon me draw souls to the kingdom of God in the name of Jesus.

41. O God arise and let my heaven open for signs and wonders in the name of Jesus.

42. Powers nursing sickness in my body expire, in the name of Jesus.

43. Miracle blockers be silenced in the name of Jesus.

44. Evil structure around me, I pull you down, in the name of Jesus.

45. Divine anointing of deliverance flow in my life, in the name of Jesus.

46. My organs, receive creative miracle in the name of Jesus.

47. Anointing of God on my head, direct miracle hijackers elsewhere in the name of Jesus.

48. I shall not die unfruitful and unfulfilled in the name of Jesus.

49. Anointing of God make me a product of possibility of greatness in the name of Jesus.

50. Every frustration in my life, become a bridge to my miracle, in the name of Jesus.

51. Anointing of God upon me, disgrace my stubborn problems in the name of Jesus.
52. My rising sun shall not go down in the name of Jesus.
53. Signs and wonders appear in my life, in the name of Jesus.

CHAPTER 6

THANKSGIVING IN THE MOUTH OF LIONS

Thanksgiving is powerful than prayer. It is not petition but testimony of what God did. You are not asking God anything but thanking him. It is time of joy and telling God, he did everything no other gods did. Thanksgiving is food God feeds. He loves being thanked every hour and every day. Thanksgiving is the one most potent advantage you have as Christian. When you give thanks, God is left loose to show his power and Excellency. Some things are more powerful than prayer, thanksgiving is one. Instead of dealing with the mountain sometimes, thank God. As you thank him he doesn't say anything but watch from his seat and smile wishing you better in his adoration. The lion spirit in you awakes and is happy. The lion spirit in you awakes and strategizes. The Lion triggers in you and its mouth full of thanksgiving.

The angels arouse and surround you because you give thanks to God. You won't speak to mountain before it moved or flattened. Barriers are broken. Pits are filled up. Wonders begin to happen at the same time. Without human connection the hands of God begins to manipulate things. You step into wealth, step into abundance and step into breakthrough. People will look at you and testify, you don't look like what you use to be. They see you as ordinary in the past, but now seen as kingdom commander. Something supernatural happens in your life. The spirit of Lion in you create atmosphere for it. Therefore, open your heart wide and move forward by fire.

O give thanks to the Lord for the Lord is good. Give thanks to God all the time. Count your blessings, name them one by one. When you begin to see what God has done, name them one by one. Is it bareness of many years that is gone?, mention it because now you are with biological baby

/children around with joy. You are happy. Is it finance, you lost your job or business is not ok, but now life changes and you rent good apartment or now a landlord or landlady. Was your son or daughter doing drug but now free of it because God take control? Thank God. Is it your marriage? Domestic violence every day! Neighbors make jest of you, but now good breeze take over your home and there is peace. You smile to office. Smile to market, smile to church, and smiles all over you! Thank God. Your destiny is ruled by Lion of the tribe of Judah.

Do you know, you may have been in prison today? You may have been in the mortuary today, but how God brought you out, is miraculous. Give thanks all the time. Do you ever sit down one day, thank God and say, "O Lord, look how dependable you are". It is the mercy of God that you do business and someone think good of you in this wicked and be-deviled world. Look at how far you have gone in life; forget about having millions or not in your bank account. That you are alive is enough. Demons have destroyed many but you are not. God delivered you in a miraculous way. You need to thank God.

Satan is not on holiday but God keep you save. Do you think it is easy? Many homes were swept by torrents of dark flood. Thunder strikes and consumed families but you are alive with your family. You live in Goshen; land of plenty without sickness. The Lion of Judah keep you save. You can see the marvelous hand work in your life. You have roof above your head and have pleasant sleep.

You hear of kidnapping and even know people kidnap around you, yet you are not kidnapped. What about rituals foot soldiers around? Many left home but never return. You were not a victim. Thank God! What about the transformation of your mind? You don't think irrational but straight.

When you talk, people give you applause. You speak with wisdom in the like of King Solomon a man loaded with wisdom. People love to listen to you. You can see the way of God and see the kingdom clearer.

There is power in thanksgiving. Thanksgiving releases fresh oil. That you pick this book, fresh oil is coming on you. Why do you need fresh oil? This is what the bible says: ***"And it shall come to pass in that day, that his burden shall be taken away from off thy shoulder, and his yoke from off thy neck and the yoke shall be destroyed because of the anointing."* Isaiah 10:27.** Fresh oil destroys yoke of darkness. Yokes make you stagnant, sick, poor and backward.

Anointing is of God. You can't have it if God refuses to give you. Divine anointing is positive and is loaded with breakthrough on all sides. One major way to have it is to go to God with thanksgiving. David received anointing of God because he knows how to thank him. Anytime you thank God, he stretched hands of oil to pour it on you. Ever thankful is ever anointed. Anointing is never too much.

"But my horn shalt thou exalt like the horn of a unicorn: I shall be anointed with fresh oil." **Psalm 92:10.** Anointing is a weapon that we need to silence works of darkness. When anointed by God, Satan flees. Pray for God to find you in the order of David.

***"I have found David my servant; with my holy oil have I anointed him: With whom my hand shall be established: mine arm also shall strengthen him. The enemy shall not exact upon him; nor the son of wickedness afflict him. And I will beat down his foes before his face, and plague them that hate him. But my faithfulness and my mercy shall be with him: and in my name shall his horn be exalted."* Psalm 89:20-24.**

The void of thanksgiving is void of anointing. If you need daily anointing then do daily thanksgiving. Anointing flows in the arena of thanksgiving. It flows and flows. Let your head full of anointing. Let your garment full of anointing. Let your body full of anointing. Because of the anointing of God upon you no enemy shall stand before you

Thanksgiving provokes God to take over our battle. Let the cup of your anointing full before the Lord. Let it over flow to operate in the radar of heaven so that your ears may hear the desire of the wicked that rise up against you. The wicked shall fall and not rise. They shall cripple and not walk. Every battle is a relay race. As you thank God, you give God the baton as in a relay race, moving forward as you do. He takes over from there. When he take over, you start not worrying because he is in charge and he never fail.

You war in prayer, you watch in thanksgiving *"And Moses said unto the people, fear ye not, stand still, and see the salvation of the Lord, which he will show to you today; for the Egyptians whom ye have seen today, ye shall see them no more forever."* **Exodus 14:13.** With anointing of God upon the Israelites they were saved and saw the salvation. They watch the Egyptians drowned in the Red Sea. Anytime you are thanking and praising God, what you are saying is "O Lord, take over" "O Lord, take over every aspect of my life". I pray, the Lord Almighty will take over your battle. We seize to war to watch. When other are worry, caught with fear and tremble, a man of anointing smiles and trust in the Lord.

When God takes over it not only surprise you, He turns you into surprise. People look you with awe and everything in you become awesome. If you want to work pray, if you want to watch give God thanks. Don't allow thanksgiving leave your mouth. Let the spirit in you know how to praise God. Let your body be of praise. Let your hands praise God. Let your legs praise God. Let your mouth praise God and speak thanksgiving!

There is no man that can do anything without God. To those that are sons of light nothing happen that is coincidence. It is hand of God that makes things happen. In Mark 16:20, it is written, And they went forth, and preached everywhere, the Lord working with them, and confirming the word with signs following. Amen. The Apostles know they heal, it is not by their power. They make paralytic walk, they know it is not by their power. They open the eyes of the blind, they knew it is not by their power. They prophesy, they knew it wasn't their prophecy that makes things happen. It was God's power and confirmation and ruling in the situation. This is the reason Paul said in **1 Corinthians 3: 6-7:** *"I have planted, Apollos* *watered; but God gave the increase. So then neither is he that planteth anything, neither he that watereth; but God that giveth".* Without God's impute in the equation everything will is mire activities. The bible says those who build, build in vain unless God's hand is in it. You may have connection yet you don't progress.

Thanksgiving is paramount in the mouth of who knows its value. There are people in precarious condition that lose hope and pray God to see them through. They lost hope and never belief they can overcome it. Some are poor while some need God or healing; some are barren for many years while some are ripe in age but no partner to marry. People in this condition always look at a day that will overcome the situation and thank God. Such people hesitate for answer or deliverance. But, there are situations they receive healing, became rich and marry the bone of their bone. They easily forget what they passed through in the past.

The book of **Psalm 103:1-5 says:** *"Bless the LORD, O my soul: and all that is within me, bless his holy name. Bless the LORD, O my soul, and forget not all his benefits: who forgiveth all thine iniquities; who healeth all thy diseases; who redeemeth thy life from destruction; who crowneth thee with lovingkindness and tender mercies; who satisfieth thy mouth with good things; so that thy youth is renewed like the eagle's."*

Also, the book of **Isaiah 48:21** gives part of the summary. *"And they did not thirst when He led them through the deserts; he caused the waters to flow from the rock for them; he also split the rock, and the waters gushed out."* You won't suffer thirst. Water flows around you and you lack nothing. You plantations are nourished with heavenly water. You get your fruits at season. You have no cause to complain. Fruitfulness is your watchword.

We thank God for continuous increase of the word. The more you raise thanksgiving songs to God, the more he hears you and more you are happy. What you think is full suddenly increases. Your heart is full of joy. *"And the word of God increased; and the number of the disciples multiplied in Jerusalem greatly; and a great company of the priests were obedient to the faith."* **Acts 6:7.**

We thank God for divine speed who gives special speed. He gives speed of operation in what to do. He gives the speed of success; the speed of breakthrough; the speed of climbing and not to fall and the speed of Elijah to overtake Ahab. Elijah was happy to overcome worshippers of Baal. God did not only protect him, but ensure he soar like eagle. This is not common. *"Then the LORD gave special strength to Elijah. He tucked his cloak into his belt and ran ahead of Ahab's chariot all the way to the entrance of Jezreel."* **1 kings 18:46.** This is an old man on feet that run and overtake Ahab on horse. He beat Ahab, clean. You belong to family where hands of God are at work. You won't fail but succeed. Speed will ever be on your side. You will overtake your enemies and be above them. They will see your back and not overtake you in the race of greatness. You will not fall or be disgraced, in the name of Jesus.

We thank God for continuous supply in everything we do. His source of supply never dries. When it seems stagnation or retard is about to show its ugly face, God appears on the scene to surprise you. It is investment upon investment, no borrowing, no bank loan, no overdraft. Instead of stagnation, massive projects go on.

When you thank God, he releases prophecies into you. What God says can't come back void. As he pronounces it, so it goes wide and far. God says it, God fulfills it. He has overall power to fulfill what he says. It is not our concern to struggle and fulfill his words. Is his hand too short to fulfill it? No, neither does he lose sight to fulfill it? No. neither does he lack strength to fulfill what he says. The prophecy he releases, he fulfills!

For those who know the meaning and value of thanksgiving stick to it. No matter the distance to helpers they search for him or her. A good example is one of the ten healed by Jesus. The lepers had something in common. The sickness of leprosy is contagious. For this reason, they are not allowed in the town. They are segregated, confuse, lonely, sorrowful and dejected. Jesus was passing by when he saw them in group. I pray, such tragedy will not be your portion. Amen. They recognize the power of Jesus. This is the reason they cry to Jesus to have mercy on them. They cry to Jesus not man. Learn to open your mouth wide and call on Jesus. Let the spirit of Lion in you wake to cry to Jesus. This is the start of deliverance from bondage of darkness. Jesus is the one that transforms life.

Jesus healed them and said they should go and show themselves to the priest in town. With Joy they went to the priest who will approve the healing. The healing was approved. They should have return to Jesus to thank him. They never did except one of them. This surprised Jesus, when he asked, where are the remaining nine? The other nine knew not the value to thanksgiving. The spirit of Lion in them slept. It never encouraged them to go back and thank Jesus. But the one that went back, Jesus said to him, he is made whole. This means perfection in healing.

A lavish gratitude in recognition to greatness and faithfulness of God is thanksgiving. The remaining nine are like many believers today. You are not grateful until you show your gratitude to the one that helped you. Let the person that helps you have the feelings that you really thank him. For example, the way you say thank you to a small help should be different from big help. If someone gives you a hundred dollar and another time a five thousand dollars, the way you smile to the first will be different to the second. In another time if he gives you twenty thousand dollars, you will appreciate beyond the first and the second times. Don't let your gratitude be minor. At all times be grateful. When you give gratitude to helper, it makes him feel he is indebted to you. He will love to do more. He is motivated to do more. The rule is, don't say, "Thank you too late". If someone helps you and it is the third day you say, "Thank you" it is too late! This may be the last he will help.

As it is to human being so is God. God want you to thank him all the time. It is not until you see physical thing, thank him all the time. The air you breathe can be free, but it is not. Don't wait till you pay for oxygen in hospital before you know the air is a luxury made free for you. That you go to toilet freely worth thanksgiving. That you raise your hands as you walk demands thanksgiving to God. You feed without aid, walk without aid, talk without aid, and see without aid of anyone or things you need.

What you don't understand is, when God do something, thank him. For doing this, he will do more next time. When God gave you tea and you roll on the ground as if he gave you a restaurant; I assure you he will give you tea and bread. God gives you tea and bread and you roll on the ground and thank Him, I assure you he will give you whole factory that makes tea and bread. If he sees you give thanks, he will say next time. I will make sure I give you people that will mix the tea and bread for you. Your level changed. What makes you appreciative is the spirit of Lion of Judah in you.

Gratitude is very powerful. Doors difficult to open won't be if you are grateful. Good doors will open to you as a result of gratitude. What someone pray and fast for can come to you as gift because you are grateful. It is not that David is special, he grow because he has the attitude of thanksgiving. The book of Psalms is loaded with thanksgiving and deliverance. If you are delivered, you end it with thanksgiving! David lavishes thanksgiving to God.

Many people are not grateful. They are not grateful to God and not grateful to men. Many are surrounded by uncles, sisters, aunts, brothers and friends. When they help and you are told to show gratitude, you say, why you should, they know your condition. You can't see anything from them again. The sad aspect of it is some people never tell their parents thank you. Some never tell their children thank you. Some never tell their spouse thank you. Some never tell their pears thank you. Some never tell their boss thank you. If you don't have the habit to say thank you, it is a big attack. The arrogant statement they say is, "Why should I tell anyone that help me, thank you?" My parents perform their duty. My friend is my friend we see every day. I don't count it necessary. This attitude makes you cancel opportunity. My advice is, be thankful to your benevolent. It is a sign of maturity and responsibility. In every situation, have the habit of saying, "Thank you".

Awake the spirit of Judah in you to thank God and flourish like the palm tree. Your story is supernatural if your life becomes like palm tree. There is no part of palm tree that is not useful. Palm tree is ever green no matter the weather or climate. The root goes deep, into the soil to tap deep resources beyond other trees. This means, in the order of palm tree, you tap deep into whatever you want or need. And because of anointing bumper harvest awaits you. ***"The righteous shall flourish like the palm tree: he shall grow like a cedar in Lebanon. Those that be planted in the house of the LORD shall flourish in the courts of our God." Psalm 92:12-13.***

I prophesy to your life, from this day you shall flourish to life. Be ever thankful. You are ever fruitful like the palm tree. In everything you lay hands, you will be fruitful, in business, in career, in marriage etc. In every position you meet yourself always thank God. When you wake in the morning, the first word in your mouth should be, "Thank you Jesus" and let the last word in your mouth as you go to sleep be, "Thank you Jesus".

Be a party to brethren's called ever thankful ever-rising. They use thanksgiving as weapon of grace. The more you give thanks to the Lord, better you rise. Their motor is, ever jumping, ever going up. Nothing goes down for thanks giver. They excel and never go down. You never meet a thanks giver where you meet him. Before you arrive he has changed level. He changed level every day, every week, every month, every year and every season. From today, this will be your tradition and life style in the name of Jesus. You don't suffer demotion for thanking God. Thank him and continue to thank him.

Don't wait for signs to praise, you praise to see the signs. Do you want to see signs?, have the capacity of praising God. Rejoice in the Lord always. Rejoice opens great doors even when there is no sign of breakthrough but knows, with God all things are possible. As you praise God, he is your strength. You walk upon your high places.

You grow daily; let your mouth full of thanksgiving. It enable you grow till old age. Thanksgiving won't allow you diminish in age, diminish in strength, and diminish in memory, but not so with thanksgiving. Ever thanking ever strengthened. At old age you shall bring mental fruit, spiritual fruit, and physical fruit at old age. This is what Sarah has at old age. Abraham and Sarah delivered Isaac.

We must be conscious of not giving thanks. Ingratitude is a risk. Lack of thanksgiving can turn our glory to shame. You believe you are famous because of your strength, wisdom and understand. Who gives strength, Knowledge, Wisdom and understanding? It is God who gives all. If you don't praise God, he will curse your blessings. It won't yield if you boast about. Boast derail men and women. Praise God rather than boast about and around.

When people have money in the bank in millions they boast rather than give thanks to God. They boast, "I can't go down again" They bury money underground. Keep them in water tanks and sealed boreholes. They burry hopes of people in the ground! The money that supposed to be shared or given out to less privileged or to people who are hungry is buried in the ground. They thank God but it is empty thanksgiving. To some, when they boast and invest, the money vanished because they believe it is their strength. Anything they depend on God ensures it fails. ***"Behold, I will corrupt your seed, and spread dung upon your faces, even the dung of your solemn feasts; and one shall take you away with it."*** **Malachi 2:3.** I pray may your glory not turn to shame. Amen

Lack of thanksgiving can stop your way forward. You rotate in the same axis and find it difficult to rise. It can get you stalled. It can bring stagnation to man. Whatever God provides, don't despise it. Life is a matter of one step after another. Rome was not built in a day. Have reason to praise God every day. Are you in one room apartment? Don't despise God and say, "What is this". You have a small car, don't say, "What is this". Nothing moves forward when you ask the question, "What is this?" Let your tongue praise God all the time.

Lack of thanksgiving can lead you to captivity. Your mouth either opens the way or captivates you. *"Hear ye, and give ear; be not proud: for the*

LORD hath spoken. Give glory to the LORD your God, before he cause darkness, and before your feet stumble upon the dark mountains, and, while ye look for light, he turn it into the shadow of death, and make it gross darkness." **Jeremiah 13:15-16.**

Avoid pride it sinks life and destiny. Fall goes before the pride. Failure to thank God is imprisonment without knowing. Where you call bus stop, is the beginning of glory, but you call

Lack of thanksgiving open door to destruction. I pray you shall not be destroyed. When you thank God, he gives you discernment to know the good and the bad. Destructive plantation takes over the life of people that doesn't know how to praise God.

PRAYER POINTS

1. Thank you Jesus for the opportunity I have to thank you, in the name of Jesus.
2. I thank God; his testimony is in my mouth, in the name of Jesus.
3. I am before you Lord, to thank you on and forever in the name of Jesus.
4. I thank you doing for me what other gods can't do, in the name of Jesus.
5. O Lord, you don't eat physical food, but thanksgiving, I thank you Lord, receive my thanksgiving.
6. O Lord, thank you for empowering me, thank you for every hour, every day of my life, in the name of Jesus.
7. I thank God who makes himself available for me always.
8. I thank God for showing his excellence to strengthen me.

9. I thank Jesus, for washing me clean with his precious blood.
10. I thank God for feeding me with his blood to flush me of evil deposit.
11. I thank God for feeding me with his blood to make me whole within and without.
12. I thank Jesus for immunizing me with his blood against sickness and diseases, in the name of Jesus.
13. I thank Jesus for immunizing me with his blood against evil arrow.
14. I thank Jesus for protecting me with his blood.
15. I thank Jesus who comforts me with his blood.
16. I thank Jesus who allows me to be bold like Lion before my enemy.
17. I thank God who watches me on his seat and smile at me as approval of father and son/daughter in the name of Jesus
18. I thank my God who makes the lion in me awake to face daily challenges.

19. I thank God, with you barriers are broken, in the name of Jesus
20. I thank my God, with him on my side, every evil pit dug for me are filled up.
21. Angels of God arouse and surround me in the name of Jesus.
22. I thank God, with him on my side, I step to breakthrough.
23. O Lord, I thank you of supernatural hands you laid upon me for signs and wonders.
24. O Lord, I thank you for silencing spirit of bareness in my family in the name of Jesus
25. I thank my God who opens great doors of blessing to my life.
26. I thank God who rules me by the spirit of Lion of Judah that never fail.
27. Lord Jesus, I thank you for keeping my accounts save in the name of Jesus
28. Lord Jesus, thank you for keeping me save from demons of destruction in the name of Jesus

29. I thank God; I shall live in plenty, in the name of Jesus.
30. I thank God for providing me with shelter, in the name of Jesus.
31. I thank God; I am not kidnapped, in the name of Jesus.
32. I thank God for his transformation of my mind, in the name of Jesus.
33. I thank you Lord of the wisdom deposited in my life.
34. I thank you Lord of the fresh oil poured on me, in the name of Jesus.
35. I thank God, anointing breaks the yoke in your name.
36. I thank his anointing upon me silence works of darkness in my life.
37. I thank God who wears me garment of anointing in the name of Jesus.
38. I thank God who scatter and destroy powers behind my battle in the name of Jesus.

39. I thank God who destroy stubborn pursuer of my destiny.

40. Smiles of surprise; smiles of breakthroughs and favor is my portion in the name of Jesus

41. My hands are full of praises, in the name of Jesus.

42. My legs are full of praises and dance and walk in the name of Jesus

43. My mouth is full of thanksgiving; I sing and speak good things of the Lord.

44. I thank God, I flourish like the palm tree, in the name of Jesus.

45. I give thanks to God, in everything I lay hands upon, I shall prosper in the name of Jesus

46. I thank God who uphold me against failure and debt in the name of Jesus

47. I thank God who makes me to soar like the eagle in the name of Jesus.

48. Lord Jesus, thank you for my thirst and hunger for prayer.

49. I thank God, I don't suffer memory loss in the name of Jesus
50. I thank God; he is my strength and benefactor in the name of Jesus
51. O Lord, I thank you for expelling spirit of captivity in my life in the name of Jesus
52. I thank God who turns stagnation in my life to breakthrough in the name of Jesus
53. I thank God, he never allow my glory turn to shame in the name of Jesus
54. Act of thanksgiving shall not leave my family in the name of Jesus
55. I rise and shine because I give thanks to the Lord in the name of Jesus.

YOU HAVE BATTLES TO WIN
TRY THESE BOOKS

1. <u>COMMAND THE DAY: DAILY PRAYER BOOK</u>

Each day of the week is loaded with meanings and divine assurance. God did not create each day of the week for the fun of it. Blessings, success, gifts, resources, hopes, portfolios, duties, rights, prophecies, warnings and challenges, are loaded in each day.

Do you know the language, command or decree you can use to claim what belongs to you in each day of the week? Do you know in Christendom, Monday can be equated to one of the days of creation in Genesis chapter one? Do you know creation lasted for six days and God rested on the seventh day? What day of the week can Christian equate as the first day of the week, if we follow Christian calendar? What day can we call day seven?

This book shall give insight to these questions. It shall explain how you can command each day of the week according to creation in the book of Genesis chapter one.

Above all, you shall exercise your right and claim what is hidden in each day of the week.

Check for this in **COMMAND THE DAY: DAILY PRAYER BOOK**

2. PRAYER TO REMEMBER DREAMS

A lot of people are passing through this spiritual epidemic on a daily basis. Their dream life is epileptic, having no ability to remember all dreams they dream, or sometimes forget everything entirely. This is nothing but spiritual havoc you need to erase from your 0spiritual record.

The answer to every form of spiritual blackout caused by spiritual erasers is found in, **PRAYER TO REMEMBER DREAMS**

3. 100% CONFESSIONS AND PROPHECIES TO LOCATE HELPERS AND HELPERS TO LOCATE YOU

This is a wonderful book on confessions and prophecies to locate helpers and helpers to locate you. It is a prayer book loaded with over two thousand (2,000) prayer points.

The book unravels how to locate unknown helpers, prayers to arrest mind of helpers and prayers for manifestation after encounter with helpers.

4. ANOINTING FOR ELEVENTH HOUR HELP: HOPE AND HELP FOR YOUR TURBULENT TIMES

This book tells much of what to do at injury hour called eleventh hour. When you read and use this book as prescribed fear shall vanish in your life when pursuing a project, career or contract.

5. PRAYER TO LOCATE HELPERS AND HELPERS TO LOCATE YOU

Our divine helper is God. He created us to be together and be of help to one another. In the midst of no help we lost out, ending our journey in the wilderness.

There are keys assign to open right doors of life. You need right key to locate your helpers. Enough is enough; of suffering in silence.

With this book, you shall locate your helpers while your helpers shall locate you.

6. FIRE FOR FIRE PART ONE: (PRAYER BOOK BOOK 1)

This prayer book is fast at answering spiritual problems. It is a bulldozer prayer book, full of prayers all through. It is highly recommended for night vigil. Testimonies are pouring in daily from users of this book across the world!

7. PRAYER FOR FRUIT OF THE WOMB: EXPECTING MOTHERS

This prayer book is children magnet. By faith and believe in God Almighty, as soon as you use this book open doors to child bearing shall be yours. Amen

8. PRAYER FOR PREGNANT WOMEN: WITH ALL CHRISTIAN NAMES AND MEANINGS

This is a spiritual prayer book loaded with prayers of solution for pregnant women. As soon as you take in, the prayers you shall pray from day one of conception to the day of delivery are written in this book.

9. WARFARE IN THE OFFICE: PRAYER TO SILENCE TOUGH TIMES IN OFFICE

It is high time you pray prayers of power must change hands in office. Use this book and liberate yourself from every form of office yoke.

10. MY MARRIAGE SHALL NOT BREAK: THE SECRET TO LOVE AND MARRIAGE THAT LASTS

Marriage is corner piece of life, happiness and joy. You need to hold it tight and guide it from wicked intruders and destroyer of homes.

11. VICTORY OVER SATANIC HOUSE PART ONE: RIDDING YOUR HOME OF SPIRITUAL DARKNESS

Are you a tenant, Land lord bombarded left and right, front and back by wicked people around you?

With this book you shall be liberated from the hooks of the enemy.

12. DICTIONARY OF DREAMS: THE DREAM INTERPRETATION DICTIONARY WITH SYMBOLS, SIGNS, AND MEANINGS

THE LION OF THE TRIBE OF JUDAH

This is a must book for every home. It gives accurate details to about **10,000 (Ten thousand) dreams and interpretations,** written in alphabetical order for quick reference and easy digestion. The book portrays spiritual revelations with sound prophetic guidelines. It is loaded with Biblical references and violent prayers.

Ask for yours today.

TELLA OLAYERI

For Further Enquiries Contact
THE AUTHOR
EVANGELIST TELLA OLAYERI
P.O. Box 1872 Shomolu Lagos.
Tel: +2348023583168

FROM AUTHOR'S DESK

BEFORE YOU GO

Hello,

Thank you for purchasing this book. Would you consider posting a review about this book? In addition to providing feedback and arousing others into Christ's bosom, reviews can help other customers to know about the book.

Please take a minute to leave a review on this book.

I would appreciate that!

Thank you in advance, for your review and your patronage!!

If you would like to leave a review on my other books click the link below.

https://tellaolayeri.com/review.php

NOTE: You can get all my books from my website **www.tellaolayeri.com**

SHARE YOUR TESTIMONY

We love testimonies. We love to hear what God has done for you, your family, your business etc. as you draw close to Him in prayer. Please share your testimony with us.

https://tellaolayeri.com/testimony.php

NOTE: If you want your picture to be shown with your testimony send it to **tellaolayeri@gmail.com**

I also invite you to checkout our website at **www.tellaolayeri.com** and consider joining our newsletter (get free six powerful book) which we send out once in a while with great tips, testimonies and revelations from God's Word for a victorious living.

Feel free to drop us your prayer request. We will join faith with you and God's power will be released in your life and issue in question.

www.tellaolayeri.com/prayerrequest.php

GOOD NEWS!!!

My audiobook is now available, to get one visit **audible**.

If you are reading from my paperback visit **acx.com** and search **"Tella Olayeri."**

Brethren, to be loaded and reloaded visit: **amazon.com/author/tellaolayeri** for a full spiritual sojourn for my books.

Thanks.

THE LION OF THE TRIBE OF JUDAH

DONATE TO THE MINISTRY

Why Give?

We have two major area of focus: The less Privileged and Charity.

Service to people and help to set up outstanding Modern Printing Press to reach thousands for free evangelism pamphlets and books to hinterland and the needy.

To achieve this, financial support is needed and we count you as one to support this ministry. A drop of water makes an ocean.

No donation is small or little. Donate through any of the ways listed below. May God bless your purse and source. Amen.

DONATE IN NAIRA

Bank Name: Guaranty Trust Bank Plc.

Account Name: OLAYERI ADIKU TELLA

Account Number: 0499255414

DONATE IN DOLLARS

Bank Name: Guaranty Trust Bank Plc.

Account Name: OLAYERI ADIKU TELLA

Account Number: 0499255098

Swift code: GTBINGLA

Visit the donation page on my website to donate online:

www.tellaolayeri.com/donate.php

ABOUT THE AUTHOR

Tella Olayeri grew from Spiritual Warrior to Spiritual Warlord in the Vineyard of God. His books have changed lives of millions, with banner of praises and testimonies in their hands!

He is a solution giver to problems and challenges men and women pass through on daily basis. He frowns at satanic oppression and demonic agenda propagated by powers of darkness. He is known for his wonderful deliverance books that address, swallow and bring abrupt end to fierce attacks of the enemy. **"Wonders and miracles"**, connotes his deliverance books.

Tella's books are globally read and accepted, based on operation "do-it-yourself". His books are instant solution to problems laced with fire prayer missiles that give instant deliverance to demonic yoke and oppression, health hazards, witchcraft attacks etc. His books will teach your hands to wage war and your fingers to fight against forces of darkness.

Tella Olayeri is a role model in Christian warfare. He is a Counselor and Preacher of the Word. His writings are wonderful and courageous for Christian soldiers in the battle of life to harvest breakthrough, salvation, spiritual protection, open doors and miracles.

One of his major research book is **DICTIONARY OF DREAMS**, that gives instant relief to millions of how to interpret dreams. The book has about ten thousand (10,000) dreams with accurate interpretations.

Tella Olayeri is happily married to his wife, Sister Ngozi Judith Olayeri. The marriage is blessed with five children, Miss Ibukun, David, Michael, Miss Comfort and Miss Mercy.

Connect with Tella Olayeri at **www.tellaolayeri.com** to receive powerful daily message.

Printed in Great Britain
by Amazon